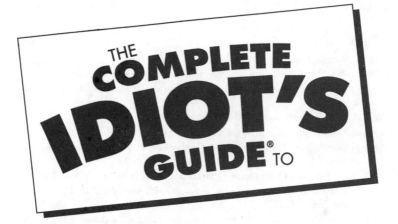

Dog Tricks

D0029143

by Liz Palika

ALPHA

A member of Penguin Group (USA) Inc.

ALPHA BOOKS

Published by the Penguin Group

Penguin Group (USA) Inc., 375 Hudson Street, New York, New York 10014, U.S.A.

Penguin Group (Canada), 10 Alcorn Avenue, Toronto, Ontario, Canada M4V 3B2 (a division of Pearson Penguin Canada Inc.)

Penguin Books Ltd, 80 Strand, London WC2R 0RL, England

Penguin Ireland, 25 St Stephen's Green, Dublin 2, Ireland (a division of Penguin Books Ltd)

Penguin Group (Australia), 250 Camberwell Road, Camberwell, Victoria 3124, Australia (a division of Pearson Australia Group Pty Ltd)

Penguin Books India Pvt Ltd, 11 Community Centre, Panchsheel Park, New Delhi—110 017, India

Penguin Group (NZ), cnr Airborne and Rosedale Roads, Albany, Auckland 1310, New Zealand (a division of Pearson New Zealand Ltd)

Penguin Books (South Africa) (Pty) Ltd, 24 Sturdee Avenue, Rosebank, Johannesburg 2196, South Africa

Penguin Books Ltd, Registered Offices: 80 Strand, London WC2R 0RL, England

Copyright © 2005 by Liz Palika

International Standard Book Number: 1-59257-399-1
Library of Congress Catalog Card Number: 2005925425

07   06   05   8   7   6   5   4   3   2   1

Interpretation of the printing code: The rightmost number of the first series of numbers is the year of the book's printing; the rightmost number of the second series of numbers is the number of the book's printing. For example, a printing code of 05-1 shows that the first printing occurred in 2005.

Printed in the United States of America

Note: This publication contains the opinions and ideas of its author. It is intended to provide helpful and informative material on the subject matter covered. It is sold with the understanding that the author and publisher are not engaged in rendering professional services in the book. If the reader requires personal assistance or advice, a competent professional should be consulted.

The author and publisher specifically disclaim any responsibility for any liability, loss, or risk, personal or otherwise, which is incurred as a consequence, directly or indirectly, of the use and application of any of the contents of this book.

Most Alpha books are available at special quantity discounts for bulk purchases for sales promotions, premiums, fund-raising, or educational use. Special books, or book excerpts, can also be created to fit specific needs.

For details, write: Special Markets, Alpha Books, 375 Hudson Street, New York, NY 10014.

Publisher: *Marie Butler-Knight*
Product Manager: *Phil Kitchel*
Senior Managing Editor: *Jennifer Bowles*
Senior Acquisitions Editor: *Mike Sanders*
Development Editor: *Michael Thomas*
Production Editor: *Janette Lynn*
Copy Editor: *Molly Schaller*

Illustrator: *Chris Eliopoulos*
Photography: *Sheri Wachtstetter*
Cover/Book Designer: *Trina Wurst*
Indexer: *Angie Bess*
Layout: *Becky Harmon*
Proofreading: *John Etchison*

Contents at a Glance

Contents

Foreword

Many years ago I taught a basic Household Pet Obedience class. The goal was to have dogs learn the basic obedience commands to make them better pets. We practiced waiting at doors, sitting while a bowl was put down, etc. I added a trick each week to make the class fun.

At the end of the six weeks, *every* dog in my class could perform *every* trick, though about half of them were not doing their basic commands. The tricks were often much more complicated than the commands.

This made me realize a couple of things. First, if the people think it's fun, they will work hard at teaching their dogs. Second, when the people are having fun, the dogs will have more fun. Overall, the tricks helped much more to cement the family bond with the dogs than the "useful" basic obedience commands. Families are much more tolerant of a dog who shreds toilet paper if that dog also speaks on command, sits up, and rolls over.

If a dog is well behaved, he is much more likely to live out his life as a beloved family member.

This is where Liz's book becomes invaluable. As an instructor and rescue person, Liz knows firsthand how important it is to integrate a dog fully into a family. One of the best ways is through fun and games such as dog tricks. This book starts with some very basic tricks and runs all the way up to housecleaning! Okay, so housecleaning is a slight exaggeration, but picking up toys is a skill many of us work tirelessly to teach our children, let alone our dogs.

The Complete Idiot's Guide to Dog Tricks gives careful, step-by-step directions to help you teach your dog and warns of pitfalls and possible problems along the way. Liz also suggests ways to make doing tricks an important part of your dog's day—making your dog a better canine citizen as well as a fun-loving family member. I took the section on having your dog pick up his toys and followed the steps with two of my own dogs—my ten-month-old puppy and my mature six-year-old dog. Within just a couple of days I had both dogs picking up their toys. Now I need to try her technique on my two children!

I like the easy-to-use format of this book and the way I can pick it up, figure out a trick to try this week, and quickly follow the steps. Once basic tricks are mastered, Liz gives you additional ideas to keep the tricks fresh in your dog's mind and keep both of you interested. I definitely feel this book is a wonderful addition to any dog owner's library as well as for instructors, 4-H leaders, and community libraries. It has a prominent place on a shelf in our kitchen, with easy access for quick tricks.

—Deb M. Eldredge, DVM, award-winning veterinarian, dog trainer, and author

Introduction

Have you ever walked out to the curb to get your morning newspaper, in your robe with your hair messed up, and been embarrassed when a neighbor greets you? Why go through that embarrassment? Send your dog out for the paper while you stand safely inside the front door!

Trick training is great fun, cements a strong relationship with your dog, and has a few practical applications as well—such as allowing you to hide while your dog gets the morning paper. Trick training can be an icebreaker, too, by making people laugh. Therapy dog owners know that even a simple trick like Shake or Bow can get people talking about the dog, thus making a therapy dog visit more effective.

The Complete Idiot's Guide to Dog Tricks is exactly what the title says, a complete book about teaching dog tricks. There are over fifty tricks taught here, plus variations of several that can make them look different. As the owner of Kindred Spirits Dog Training in Vista, California, I have long encouraged dog owners to incorporate fun training into their basic obedience training. When you have fun with your dog, and enjoy your training, you will be more likely to continue doing it. And with dog training, practice does make perfect!

The techniques taught here emphasize positive training skills. There will be no rough stuff—no harsh dog training techniques. I want you and your dog to enjoy your training time together. I want you to laugh and your dog to be eager to cooperate. However, even though positive techniques will be taught, this is not a book that teaches dog owners how to use a clicker; there are several of those books already available, and there is no need to duplicate efforts. These techniques can be used with a clicker, though, if you are already skilled in its use.

Trick training requires a foundation of the basic obedience skills, including Sit, Down, Stay, Stand, and Heel. **Part 1, "Building a Foundation,"** will teach you how to teach your dog, help you decide upon a training technique suitable for both you and your dog, and help you build the basic foundation before you begin trick training. If your dog has already been through basic obedience training, a refresher is never a bad idea. In Part 1, I will also help you set some realistic goals for your training, taking into consideration your dog's abilities, size, and body type.

Part 2, "Building-Block Tricks," introduces some easy tricks that begin with the basic obedience commands. By starting with these simple commands, you will learn how to teach tricks and your dog will gain confidence in doing them. After all, something as silly as waving a paw or rolling over is very different from Sit and Stay! But after you and your dog master a few simple tricks, you'll be ready to move on to some more complicated ones.

In **Part 3, "Tricks for Canine Geniuses,"** I will show you how to teach some more complicated tricks. But don't worry; these are not just for super geniuses! Most dogs (and dog owners) can master these with time and practice. One of my favorite tricks is the A-B-C trick. My five-year-old Australian Shepherd, Riker, is a therapy dog, and he and I regularly visit a day care for special-needs children. Because Riker can identify by name his A, B, and C blocks (as well as X, Y, Z, 1, 2, and 3), the teachers use him as a motivator for the kids. Thus, not only can Riker and I astound people when he touches the A block, but he can also help children learn to read.

In **Part 4, "Showstoppers!"** you will learn how to use your trick-training skills to put your dog to work around the house, finding your keys or the television remote. I'll also help you put together a trick routine so you can put on small shows for the neighborhood kids or for a therapy dog visit.

We'll also talk about costumes. This is a hot-button topic for many dog owners. They feel the dog is demeaned when wearing a costume. But I have found that when a safe, comfortable costume is introduced correctly, with positive reinforcements, and when the dog has fun wearing it, the costume is anything but demeaning. At special events such as holidays or parades, on therapy dog visits, or as part of a trick routine, costumes can add a lot of excitement.

As you read through this book, you will see that I like to have fun with my dogs. They must behave, too, of course, but I share my home with dogs because I enjoy their company, like doing things with them, and they make me laugh. I wrote this book so you can have fun with your dogs, too. So enjoy!

Who Am I?

As a dog obedience instructor with over 25 years of experience, I have answered numerous questions from dog owners who are frustrated by their dogs. They don't know why their dogs do what they do and are usually frustrated, often angry, and always at their wit's end. Their dogs often dig up the backyard, chew on the furniture, and misbehave when out in public. But living with a dog shouldn't be frustrating!

I teach dog obedience classes because I love dogs. My husband and I will celebrate our thirtieth anniversary this year, and we have shared our lives with dogs the entire time. In fact, we met through our dogs; his was not trained and mine was! We enjoy a variety of dog activities, from showing them in obedience to camping with them in the high Sierra Nevada Mountains. Our dogs are our companions, friends, confidants, and protectors.

However, when a dog is badly behaved and the dog's owner is always frustrated and angry, the relationship is not thriving. I teach the dog owner how to understand why her dog is doing what he's doing. When dog owners understand, and when they learn there is something they can do to remedy the situation, the relationship becomes salvageable and the dogs are no longer in danger of losing their homes.

I have taught all levels of obedience, from puppy classes through advanced levels of obedience, called utility. I have also taught agility classes, carting, and therapy dog training. However, my primary focus (and joy) is teaching pet owners how to train their family dogs to be well-behaved members of the family. When someone enrolls in one of my classes and says, "I took your class fifteen years ago with my first dog. She was a joy to us all her life but just passed away. We have a new puppy now and want her to be just as good a dog as our first dog was," I know then that all my efforts are worthwhile!

Decoding the Text

You don't have to be a dog-training expert to understand the text. There will be no technical gibberish of any kind, and any words that need to be defined, will be.

You will find four different kinds of sidebars throughout the book, each designed to add some additional information to the text.

 Dog Talk
These canine definitions will help you understand the information being discussed.

 Down, Boy!
Here you'll find warnings and cautions regarding your training and your dog's safety.

 Troubleshooting
These tidbits will help you work through any training trouble spots.

 Bet You Didn't Know
These boxes contain hints and tips for successful training.

Special Thanks!

Books are not written in a vacuum, especially dog training books. I would like to thank the trainers and students of Kindred Spirits Dog Training in Vista, California, and the members of the Foundation for Pet Provided Therapy, North County Chapter, for all the time and effort everyone put into teaching their dogs the tricks found in this book. I thank you, too, for all the time spent at photo sessions. (Although we did have great fun at those photo sessions, didn't we?)

I also want to thank my photographer, Sheri Wachtstetter, and her computer guru, Buddy Wachtstetter. I couldn't have done this without you both!

Kate Abbott with Gina and Walter; no one can do a hula in a grass skirt (with a dog) like Kate can.

Leslie Baker with Simba

Petra Burke with Teddy, Logan, and Shasta; thanks, Petra, for being the best friend anyone could hope to have!

Carol Clemens with Stanley

Pat Hawes with Dublin

Rick Hawes with Kelsey

Cayla Horn with Kona

Beverly Hodges with Molly and her grandkids, Natalie, Mason, Caleb, and Rebekah Hill

Carla and Todd Johnson with Jasmine and Bailey

Shar Jorgensen with Sophie

Laurette Lamontagne with Charlie Brown

Babette Lithgow with Sam

Mimi Loutrel with Sam

Carol Miller with Sadie

Liz Palika with Riker and Bashir

Joan Sellers with Alexander

Katy Silva with Jasper, Lily, and Sasha

Mike Sonstein with Suzette

Paulette Thurlow with Christopher

Joel Towart with Enzo

Buddy Wachtstetter with Hilly

Sheri Wachtstetter with Gordan

Kate Zarrella with Girl

Rancho Vista Retirement Community, Josephine Scarpace, May Kinney, William J. Lewis, and Laura Adams

Trademarks

All terms mentioned in this book that are known to be or are suspected of being trademarks or service marks have been appropriately capitalized. Alpha Books and Penguin Group (USA) Inc. cannot attest to the accuracy of this information. Use of a term in this book should not be regarded as affecting the validity of any trademark or service mark.

Part 1

Building a Foundation

In this part, I discuss training techniques and demonstrate why we do things they way we do in this book. The basic commands Sit, Down, Stay, Watch Me, Heel, Stand, and Come are taught. I show you how to teach your dog to retrieve reliably and how to teach him to work off leash.

Setting realistic goals is important. After all, it's easy to teach your dog to weave through your legs while you're walking if you have a Border Collie, but a little more difficult if you're five feet tall and have a huge Newfoundland.

Even if your dog has already had some training, don't skip these chapters; there is always more to learn!

Chapter 1

Teaching You to Train Your Dog

In This Chapter

- Training benefits all
- Choosing a training style
- Building behavior chains using training tools
- Training your individual dog

Too many dog owners think dog training consists of screaming like a drill instructor, "Sit!" and "Down!" and performing rote exercises over and over again. But training is much more than ordering one's dog around, and it certainly doesn't have to be forceful and loud. You can have fun with your dog and still get your message across. Granted, there is a time and a place for seriousness in dog training, but for the most part, training should be something you and your dog both want to do.

When you attend a dog training class or just practice the basic commands on your own, you can focus on the typical obedience commands: Sit, Down, Stay, Heel, and Come. Many training classes also help dog owners understand and solve bad behaviors, such as jumping on people, digging up the lawn, and chewing on shoes. All of these things are important, of course, but just keep in mind that training is much more than this.

Everything you do with your dog teaches him something. For example, as I sit at my desk writing these words, my five-year-old Australian Shepherd, Riker, is asleep in the doorway to my office. He knows I'm not to be disturbed while working, but he's nearby and will pop up the moment my desk chair creaks as I get up. My five-month-old Aussie, Bashir, is still in the process of learning the rules and a few minutes ago was nudging me with his nose. I didn't respond at all (because he wanted my attention) and he eventually gave up and is now chewing on a rawhide. I have just taught him that I'm not to be disturbed and that nudging me doesn't gain him the attention he wants. That's training, too.

Training Is Beneficial

Training your dog is something the two of you do together, as a team, rather than something you do to your dog. When you and your dog work together, the two of you bond more closely, learn more about each other, and deepen your relationship.

Training also builds better behavior. A trained dog is welcome places where poorly behaved dogs are excluded. A trained dog can go camping and hiking and can participate in dog sports and activities. A trained dog can volunteer as a therapy dog. A trained dog is a joy instead of a pain in the neck. The joys and benefits of training are numerous and far outweigh the time spent doing it. When done in a manner you both enjoy, training has no downside.

Bonding with Your Dog

The process of *bonding* with your dog begins as soon as you bring him home. If you have a young puppy, the process is usually very quick. If you have adopted an older dog, bonding might take a little more time, especially if the dog has been mistreated or is grieving his previous owners.

Dog Talk _____

Bonding is the attachment felt between a dog and owner who care about each other. It's a relationship; a partnership that is hard to define but easy to feel. If you look at your dog and smile, even when he's done something wrong, or silly, or bad, you've bonded with him.

The initial bond with your dog is a tentative one. Your dog doesn't know you yet, nor do you know him. To strengthen that bond, you must spend time with him and do things together. When you do, you learn what makes your dog tick, and how to teach him, work with him, and play with him. Your dog learns how to respond to you, what makes you happy, and what makes you angry. As you do things together, you build respect and trust, and the relationship you have deepens.

Bet You Didn't Know _____

Have you ever heard someone say that her dog seems able to read her mind? When your dog spends time with you, he learns to put two and two together and come to a conclusion. It's almost as if he really could read your mind. And then again, maybe he can!

But don't think bonding must all be deadly serious. No, there's nothing in the definition that says bonding with your dog, or training your dog, must be serious. I much prefer to laugh than cry, and would choose smiles over frowns any day, and I apply that to my training. *Trick training* is fun, and when you train your dog to perform tricks, you will laugh a lot. And that's good for you, for your dog, and for the relationship you share.

Dog Talk _____

Trick training is teaching your dog to do specific things that might or might not have practical applications but are fun to teach.

Building Better Behavior

Training, whether it's obedience training, training for a dog sport, or trick training, can help your dog be better behaved. The obedience commands, such as Sit, Down, Stay, and Heel, help teach him what to do when he hears those words, and that's very important. Your dog won't jump up on people when he knows to sit instead and to hold that sit when people touch him. He won't drag you down the street, choking himself and pulling your arm out of socket when he knows how to walk nicely on the leash.

Although basic obedience training is recommended for puppies, it's really not just for the young. Training should continue through the life of your dog. Just as you continue to learn, so should your dog. Not only does training keep him focused, it also keeps his mind active. If you didn't learn new things, you would stagnate; your dog can, too. Not only that, but a bored dog is more apt to get into trouble.

Tricks Make Training Fun

Trick training is fun; it's as simple as that. You can't teach your dog to roll over, say his prayers, or weave through your legs without laughing. When you laugh with your dog, you're going to have fun. The more fun you have, the more apt you will be to train some more, and the more you train, the better you both will be at it. Wow! There's no downside to that at all, is there?

Trick training will also challenge you and your dog. You will learn more about training your dog and you'll become a better dog trainer because you'll have to think through the training process. Even though I will take you step by step through each trick, you're going to have to do the actual training. Some tricks will come more easily to the two of you, and others will be more difficult. Just work through them and remember to have fun with your training even when it's challenging.

Trick Training Requires Basic Training

Teaching your dog to perform tricks requires a solid foundation of basic obedience training. Not only do many of the tricks begin with an obedience command (for example, Shake Hands begins with a Sit, and Roll over begins with a Down), but the process of training also teaches your dog how to learn. That's not to say he isn't learning something all the time (he is!), but he might not necessarily be taking in exactly what you want him to learn. And teaching him basic obedience shows him how to accept what you're teaching him.

Teaching your dog the basic skills also gives you a chance to figure out how to train your dog. It's not as easy as saying, "Fido, Sit!" and then watching him do it. As you teach your dog the basic commands, you will find out how to communicate with him so he understands what it is you want him to do. You will also have to discover what motivates him, so he wants to cooperate with you. By the time your dog is reliable with the *basic obedience commands*, the two of you should be comfortable with your training skills and will be ready to move on to trick training.

Dog Talk

The **basic obedience commands** have traditionally included Sit, Stay, Down, Heel, and Come, although many trainers also teach Watch Me and Release.

Choosing a Training Technique

There's a standing joke that says if you put a hundred dog trainers in a room together, the only thing they would agree on is that all the other trainers were wrong. Every dog trainer has his or her way of doing and teaching things, and every trainer thinks her way is best.

But every dog and every dog owner is different. It's important that you find a training technique that works for you. When dog owners call about my training classes and are a little hesitant, I invite them to come watch my classes. Then I encourage them to go watch a few other trainers' classes. They can then see which technique will

suit them best. You can also read several books and watch a variety of videos to get a feeling about other techniques.

You must be comfortable with the technique you're using. If you're not, if you're hesitant to apply it (for any reason), your dog will pick up on those emotions and won't cooperate fully. You must have confidence in what you're doing so that your dog can have confidence in you.

Using Positive Reinforcements

The training technique used in this book emphasizes positive *training tools*. There is no rough stuff here. Instead, we will be using *positive reinforcements* to help the dog learn and to build his cooperation.

> **Dog Talk**
>
> **Training tools** are things used to help teach your dog and might include a leash, your voice, food treats, and even toys.
>
> **Positive reinforcements** are things your dog likes (such as your happy praise, food treats, and toys) that can be used as training aids. You will give him these things when he performs correctly.

I don't teach clicker training in this book. The clicker is a popular positive training technique using a small noisemaker as a training tool. The clicker is an effective training tool, but it does require some specific skills to use correctly and effectively. Because there are already many books available to dog owners that teach clicker training, I won't duplicate them. However, if you're already skilled in the use of a clicker, the tricks demonstrated in this book can be taught with one. If you have never used a clicker previously, don't worry about it. You can still train your dog using positive techniques without knowing how to use a clicker.

Using Your Voice

Most dog owners find that the easiest training tool to use is their voice. You can convey different emotions by simply changing the tone of your voice. For example, using a high-pitched happy tone of voice (think of how you said, "Ice cream!" as a child), look at your dog and say his name, "Fido!" What did he do? He probably looked at you and wagged his tail. If you repeat his name, concentrating on that happy tone of voice, he will then most likely come to you, making eye contact, as if to say, "What? What are you happy about?"

Now let him relax for a few minutes and go lie down. Now look at him and using a deeper tone of voice, such as you might use when your dog gets into trouble ("Oh, bad dog!"), repeat his name. What did your dog do this time? Most dogs will pull back their ears and lower their head. If he does, ease his confusion; go pet him and apologize!

This demonstrates the power of your voice. It's a very effective training tool. Just remember, especially in the beginning, to exaggerate the happy tone of voice.

Your voice, facial expressions, petting, and food treats are all positive reinforcements.

> **Troubleshooting**
>
> BARK) If you normally have a high-pitched voice and are prone to excitement, concentrate on staying calm for several days before beginning your dog's training. You want to have a separation between your "training voice" and behavior, and your normal voice and behavior.

Offering Food Treats

Many years ago the idea of using food treats in conjunction with training was looked down upon. I think it was considered spoiling the dog, or something like that. I still hear from people in my classes, "I want my dog to work for me, not for the treats." When I explain that the giver of the treats is very important (at least as far as the dog is concerned), they usually relent.

> **Bet You Didn't Know**
>
> Always use your voice when using food treats. For example, when your dog does something correctly, praise him as he does so, "Yeah! Good boy!" and then give him the treat. Your voice marks the good behavior; the treat rewards it.

I use food treats because they get the dog's attention faster than any other single training tool available. With some good food treats, I can teach a dog to focus on me and ignore distractions in just a few moments. After he's learned to focus on me, I can then expand his learning and teach him other things. Without the food treats, training takes much longer.

Food treats are used in several ways:

- **Rewards:** When your dog does something correctly, he will be given a piece of the treat as a reward.

- **Lure:** A treat used to lead the dog through a movement or motion is called a lure. After the dog follows the lure, he is given it as a reward.

🐾 **Target:** A treat is placed on an object or in a place to show the dog he is to move to that spot or touch that object. When he gets there, he gets the treat.

🐾 **Jackpot:** When the dog does something extraordinary, or has a training breakthrough, he should be given a handful of treats or some special treats. This super-size reward is called a jackpot.

To work, the food treats must be something your dog likes. If your dog is food motivated and will eat anything he can fit in his mouth, some of his dry dog food might work. Other dogs need something a little more special, like freeze-dried liver or homemade doggy cookies.

Here are some food treat suggestions you might find in your kitchen:

🐾 Leftover meat from dinner including chicken or beef, diced into small pieces.

🐾 Cooked hamburger, with the grease blotted off.

🐾 Carrots, diced into small pieces.

🐾 Popcorn without butter or salt.

🐾 Hot dogs, cooked, sliced, and diced into small pieces.

🐾 Elbow macaroni, boiled and soft but not mushy, cooled.

🐾 Breakfast cereal, the kind without a coating of sugar.

Food treats can also be more effective if you change them; your dog might lose some enthusiasm if he gets the same treat all the time. Have a variety of treats and offer something different at each training session.

The treats should be small, easy to eat, and should not require a lot of chewing. Chewing will take up too much time during your training.

Troubleshooting

If your dog has a tendency to get chubby, cut back on his regular food a little as he's getting more training treats. You can also increase his exercise at the same time so that he works off those extra calories.

Balls, Toys, and Noisemakers

Not all dogs are motivated by food treats, and this can present a different type of training challenge. If your dog is a picky eater and turns up his nose at treats, you will need to find something that excites him, something that gets his attention. Take him to the local pet supply store and walk him up and down the aisles. Do squeaky toys get him bouncing? Does he like the stuffed dog toys that make animal sounds? Some dogs, especially the terriers, like the furry cat toys. Other dogs go crazy over tennis balls.

After you find the toy or noisemaker that gets your dog's attention, save it for your training sessions. By limiting your dog's exposure to it, you can keep it special. If your dog has it all the time, it might lose its luster; then you'll have to find something else to motivate him.

Bet You Didn't Know

If you find your dog will work better for a toy or ball than treats, use that in place of a treat while training him. To follow the directions in this book, simply substitute "toy" or "ball" when the directions call for treats.

You will use a toy or ball in much the same way as you would a treat. When your dog does what you want, give him the toy along with verbal praise. You can toss it in the air, throw the ball, or squeak the toy as you give it to him. Let him enjoy it for a moment or two and then take it back. Praise him as he lets go of it and then continue your training.

Rewards from You

You are a vital part of your dog's rewards; you are more than just the dispenser of treats and "Good boys!" Your body language, facial expressions, and touch are all a part of your dog's training.

Recently I had a student in a basic obedience class who was quite reserved. She was able to relax enough to praise her dog effectively but her dog was still guarded in her actions and was hesitant to try anything new. I joked with the woman a little, got her to laugh, and as she relaxed, so did her dog. When the woman recognized how she was inhibiting her dog, she was able to learn to control her own body language (by relaxing her shoulders, moving her arms away from her body, leaning forward, and standing easily and less rigidly) so she could help her dog.

Facial expressions are even more important than body posture. When you're training your dog, be aware of what your facial expressions are telling your dog. Picture this scenario: You're teaching your dog something new and are concentrating on the training steps. You're trying to make sure you're doing everything right, and as you concentrate, your forehead wrinkles, you bite your bottom lip, and your eyes squint. All of a sudden you find your dog backing away from you. What happened? To your dog, all those facial expressions equal a frown, and a frown means you're not happy.

You can control your facial expressions just as you can control your body postures. Enjoy your training, don't take it too seriously, and smile! When you smile and use a happy tone of voice to praise your dog, you will find yourself enjoying the training more and your facial expressions will reflect it. Your dog will be happier to work close to you and won't be as eager to pull away from you.

You can also use petting and touch as a positive reinforcement. Although petting is not the first or even the second reward (your voice and food treats take the first and second spots), it is a viable and useable reinforcement. A pat on your dog's side as you tell him,

"Yeah! Good boy! Awesome job!" is very effective. If he's getting a jackpot reward, rub his ears, scratch his neck under his collar, or just hug him close as you also reward him with praise and treats.

Timing Is Critical

The hardest part of dog training for most dog owners is understanding the timing needed so that the dog can learn. The timing of verbal praise (or the click of the clicker, if you're using one) during the initial learning stages is of utmost importance. For example, when your dog is first learning the command Sit, he must be rewarded with praise as his hips touch the ground: "Yeah! Good boy!" That teaches him that assuming that particular position is what you want him to do.

However, as his learning progresses, you then want him to understand that Sit means assume that position and hold it. So you will then postpone the praise for a second or two after his hips touch the ground before praising him. Now you are praising him for sitting and holding still for two seconds. And when he's doing that reliably, have him hold it for five seconds, and so on.

As you teach your dog each obedience exercise and trick, have a vision in your mind of what the end result should be. Work toward that with the timing of your rewards, and reward your dog accordingly.

> **Troubleshooting**
> If your timing is late, you might be rewarding behaviors you don't want. In you're in doubt, it's better to withhold a reward than reward the wrong actions.

All About Lures and Targets

As was mentioned earlier in this chapter, food treats (or toys or balls) can be used as lures and targets as well as rewards. Both of these training techniques are helpful for both obedience and trick training, as well as training for agility, carting, therapy dog work, and other dog activities.

Leading with a Lure

A lure is a really good treat or toy held in your hand. You let your dog see or smell the good thing in your hand and then encourage him to follow your hand. This hand movement helps guide your dog into position or leads him through a movement. As he does what you want him to do (by following the lure), praise him. When he completes the movement, the lure becomes a reward (let him eat the treat or play with the toy). You will use lure training in several different obedience exercises and in many of the tricks in this book.

Lures help the dog move, to do what you ask or to go where you want him to go, but you don't want to continue using the lure forever. So when teaching any particular obedience command or trick using a lure, use the treat in hand and lure the dog three times, give him a break for a few seconds (let him get up, move around, sniff the grass, and stretch), and then repeat it another three times. After another break, go through the same motions but without a treat in your hand. If he's caught on, praise and reward him with a small jackpot. If he hasn't, do it another three times with the treat.

The movement you make with the treat in your hand as you lure your dog will eventually turn into a hand signal for that obedience exercise or trick. As your dog is able to perform without following the lure, you can make the hand movement smaller, thereby reducing the broadness of the signal.

BARK **Troubleshooting**
Use a lure only as long as your dog needs it. It's a good training tool, but you want to transition to verbal commands and hand signals, or depending upon the trick, just verbal commands, as soon as you can.

Touching a Target

Target training is similar to lure training except that the treat is placed away from the dog and the dog goes to it on his own.

You can teach your dog to touch different things in target training, including your hand (see Chapter 8), a target stick, or an object that is a part of a trick or an exercise. Target training will be a part of several tricks and is very common in dog sports, especially agility training. I will explain more about target training as we teach individual obedience or tricks because the process will vary slightly with each one.

BARK **Troubleshooting**
As with lure training, you should eliminate the treat for the target as soon as your dog is able to do without it.

Use Negatives Wisely

One of the biggest debates in dog training today surrounds the use of negative reinforcements, corrections, and punishments. To discuss this, though, we need to understand what these terms mean.

Earlier in this chapter we discussed positive reinforcements. These are things your dog likes that are given to him for a good performance; they are rewards. To keep it simple, think of the equation "positive equals give."

Negative reinforcements are things that are taken away. If your dog does not give a good performance, or does not respond as you wish, you will not give him a treat nor will you give him verbal praise. Those are both negative reinforcements. Therefore, "negative equals take away."

Because negative reinforcement equals withholding something the dog wants, it can be a very effective training tool. The dog is more apt to do what is wanted because he's motivated to get the positive reinforcement. Now, just because something is a negative reinforcement doesn't mean you are angry, or physical, or harsh with your dog. You are simply withholding the positive reinforcement.

Dog owners are often confused as to what the differences are between corrections and punishments. Many think they are the same thing, but they aren't; they have totally different meanings. I prefer to think of corrections as interruptions. For example, you walk into the kitchen and find your dog's head buried in the trashcan. You tell him, loudly and abruptly, "Hey! Get out of the trash!" That's an interruption; you stopped the behavior as it happened. This can be a very effective training tool.

Punishment, on the other hand, is very different. Let's continue with the kitchen trashcan example. You walk into the kitchen, see the trashcan dumped over and trash all over the floor. Your dog is nowhere in sight so you go get him, drag him into the kitchen, shake his collar and loudly berate him for his actions. This is punishment, and it rarely ever works. It will, however, damage the relationship you have with your dog because you'll scare him and he won't understand why you're doing this to him.

You will use simple negative reinforcements (such as withholding praise and treats) often during your basic obedience training and trick training. You may use interruptions, too, as long as you concentrate on your timing. Punishments, however, should not be used.

Training Together

Training your dog is a team effort; both of you will be learning a lot. As the two of you train together, you make some discoveries about yourself. You might find that you're a pretty good dog trainer; many people take to this naturally and just need some guidance regarding the process. Or you might discover that you are more patient than you thought. Other people have a harder time and get impatient, angry, and short with their dog. If you're in this category, stop training immediately when you find yourself in this mood—step away and try to figure out why. Don't take a bad mood out on your dog. Restart your training session when you've calmed down and can treat your dog in a positive manner.

Dogs vary in the way they react to training, too. Your job as your dog's trainer is to find out how to get and keep his attention, and then keep him motivated so that the two of you can work together.

Every dog is different and reacts to training in his own way.
It's up to you to find out how to train him most effectively.

The Least You Need to Know

- Training your dog deepens the bond you share, making your relationship better.

- Both obedience training and trick training lead to better canine behavior.

- Positive reinforcements include your voice, food treats, balls, toys, and petting.

- Negative reinforcements can be useful training tools when used wisely. Never use punishment as a training tool.

Teaching the Basic Commands

In This Chapter

- 🏠 Using the basics with trick training
- 🏠 Learning a step-by-step approach
- 🏠 Teaching the basic commands
- 🏠 Tips for successful training

The basic obedience commands include Sit, Release, Down, Stay, Watch Me, Heel, and Come. These commands should be a part of every dog's vocabulary simply because they make life with a dog much easier. Life is also safer for dogs who respond reliably to these commands. But for dogs who participate in trick training or other dog activities, these basic commands are the foundation for all the other training that will follow.

All of these commands (as well as all of the trick training) will be taught using a step-by-step approach. Don't be tempted to skip ahead, even if your dog has had some previous training. Repeat each step as it's taught until your dog is ready to move on; that will help ensure reliable behavior. If your dog has already had some of this training, a refresher never hurts.

Teaching a Step-by-Step Approach

Each step will be described from the very beginning (such as "Have your dog on leash Sitting by your left side.") and will take you through one step at a time.

Follow those steps. They're proven to work; my training students have used them over and over for more than twenty years with a variety of dogs and dog breeds. The Troubleshooting boxes explain what to do when you run into a problem. If you shortcut the steps and jump ahead, your dog will not have the reinforcement of succeeding at the earlier steps and you might find him confused and unable to proceed.

Bet You Didn't Know

Introduce one new thing (obedience exercise or trick) per training session. If you introduce multiple things, your dog will be confused and not know how this new knowledge should go together.

Don't skip around, either. If you do steps 1, 2, and 3, then go to 6, find yourself in trouble and go back to 4 and 5, your dog will be very, very confused.

Keep your training sessions short and sweet, and set your dog up to succeed every time. Train two or three times per day if you can. You'll see much more progress.

Grabbing His Attention

Before you begin to train, you want to make sure you have your dog's attention. It's tough to teach him if he's watching the ceiling fan, chasing the cat, or hunting for imaginary bugs. So to begin, find some really good treats you can use as positive reinforcements. Dig out the leftover chicken or steak, or the freeze-dried liver, and dice it up into tiny pieces.

1. Fasten the leash to your dog's collar and hold it in one hand. Have some treats in the other hand.

2. Using that happy tone of voice I talked about in the first chapter, say your dog's name, "Fido!"

3. As soon as he looks at you, praise him, again in that happy tone of voice, "Good boy!" and pop a treat in his mouth.

4. Repeat for a total of five times and quit.

> **Bet You Didn't Know**
>
> Most of these exercises and tricks can be practiced in groups of five repetitions. Do something five times and then give your dog a break. If you ask him to do something more than five times, you're apt to bore him or lose his attention. Think "fascinating five"!

After you practice this exercise five times and then stop, your dog is going to watch you, follow you around, and perhaps even beg for more treats. That's okay—praise his attention but don't feed him any more treats. Not now. You wanted to get his attention and you did. Right now he's not sure what you wanted, what he was supposed to do, or what he was being praised and rewarded for, but he's curious. Good!

In fifteen minutes or whenever you can make the time, repeat the steps above. Later in the day, do it again. Repeat the steps again the next day two or three times. After several sessions, your dog should be watching you, waiting for you to pick up the leash. When you do, and he runs to you, you're ready to move on.

> **Bet You Didn't Know**
>
> Always stop every training session before your dog gets bored, or too full for another treat. Leave him wanting to do more.

Sitting Is Always First

Many behavior and control issues are based on the fact that many dogs, especially puppies and young dogs, have little self-control.

They don't think about things; they just do them. It's difficult to teach anyone—human or canine—if you first can't get him to hold still and concentrate. The Sit command, combined with the attention exercise you just read, will help your dog hold still so that you can teach him and he can learn from you. After your dog understands the Sit command, it will be the foundation for everything else you do with him, for obedience or for trick training.

Dog Talk
Sit means lower your hips to the ground, keeping your front end up, and hold still.

Teaching your dog to *Sit* is easy; teaching him to Sit and hold still is a little harder, but we'll take this in small steps and set him up to succeed.

1. With the leash on your dog, hold it in one hand and have a treat in the other.

2. Show your dog the treat. When he reaches up to sniff it, tell him, "Fido, Sit," and move the treat above his head toward his tail.

Troubleshooting
The leash on your dog can keep him from backing away from you to see where the treat is going. Keep the leash short but not tight.

3. As his head comes up, his hips will go down.

4. As his hips touch the ground, praise him, "Good to Sit!" and pop the treat in his mouth.

5. Practice a total of five times and stop for this training session.

Come back later and repeat the steps. When your dog is Sitting when he hears the command (usually after a few training sessions), delay the treat a heartbeat or two and then give it to him. This will cause him to hold still for that bit of time, changing the definition of Sit from "Move your hips to the ground" to "Move your hips to the ground and hold still for a heartbeat."

*Let your dog sniff the treat and then move it
up and back as you say, "Fido, Sit." As his
hips touch the ground, praise and reward him.*

Over the next several days, gradually increase the wait for the
treat, from a heartbeat or two to several seconds (no more than ten
seconds right now). But make
this change gradually, and only
when your dog is succeeding by
holding still. If he's bouncing up
from the Sit, withhold the treat
and praise, and the next time,
ask him to hold it for a shorter
period of time.

Bet You Didn't Know

You can increase your
dog's interest in the Sit
by asking him to Sit for
everything he wants, not just
treats but also toys, meals, petting, and play.

Teaching the Release

Your dog needs a beginning and an end to every command. The
beginning is his name, as in "Fido, Sit." This is another reason why,

Dog Talk _____
Release means "Okay, you're done now."

at the beginning of this chapter, I suggested you use his name to stimulate his interest. However, your dog also needs to know when each exercise or trick is completed, and the _Release_ command will do that.

You can introduce this as you teach your dog the Sit command.

1. With your dog in a Sit, after you have rewarded him for Sitting, tell him, "Release!" in a conversational tone of voice (rather than in the higher-pitched tone of voice used for praise).

2. Back away from your dog and lift your hands in the air. He should follow you; when he does, praise him, "Good boy!"

3. If he's hesitant to move, use his leash to gently pull him from position to show him he's allowed to move. When he takes a step, praise him.

4. After the Release, let him move around and relax for a few seconds before asking him to do anything else.

After he knows the Release and is moving on his own, use it at the end of every obedience command and trick. Using his name at the beginning and the Release at the end gives the dog clear guidance of the parameters of each command and trick.

Introducing the Sit Stay

You can begin introducing the Sit _Stay_ when your dog will Sit and hold the position for several seconds, waiting for the praise and release, without bouncing up prematurely.

Dog Talk _____
Stay means hold this position until I come back to release you.

The Sit taught your dog to move into the Sit position and to hold it for a few seconds. The Stay will teach your dog to continue to hold that position as you step away from him.

1. With the leash on your dog, held in one hand, have some treats in your pocket and one in your other hand.

2. Have your dog Sit, reward him with praise and a treat, but do not release him. Open your now-empty hand and with the palm toward your dog, tell him "Stay" in a conversational tone of voice. (Not the happy tone of voice used for praise.) Do not step away yet.

3. Wait ten seconds, praise and reward your dog, and then release him.

4. Repeat for a total of five repetitions and then give your dog a break for a few minutes. Toss the ball or rub his tummy.

When you begin a new training session, repeat numbers 1 and 2 above, but take a step away from your dog after telling him to Stay. Wait ten seconds, step back to him, praise and reward him, and release him.

Repeat for a total of five repetitions and then give your dog a break.

As you teach the Stay, increase the time, or the distance, or your position to him, but never add more than one training criteria at a time. Don't increase the time of the stay and take extra steps at the same time. When you add something new, you might also want to relax one of the older criteria.

Troubleshooting

BARK If your dog continually bounces up, do not step away from him. Instead, hold the leash close to him, or even hold his collar as you ask him to stay. Help him hold still so that he can be rewarded. Begin moving away only when he can hold the Stay command on his own.

For example, your training schedule over several days (or even over a couple of weeks) might look like this:

🏠 Increase the time to thirty seconds.

🏠 Take two steps away for twenty seconds.

🏠 Take three steps away for twenty seconds.

🏠 Take three steps away for thirty seconds.

🏠 Take two steps to the right for twenty seconds.

🏠 Take two steps to the left for twenty seconds.

Every dog progresses at a different rate. Some have trouble holding still; others are very comfortable with this command. Be patient, help your dog to succeed, and let him progress at his own speed.

Teaching the Down

The *Down* is a wonderful command that you will use around the house as well as out in public. When your dog knows how to lie down and relax, he can control his own actions, thereby preventing annoying behavior such as begging during meals or mobbing your guests. You can also have him Down and Stay when something happens and you need to control him, such as doing a Down Stay after dropping something on the kitchen floor. The Down is also the foundation for several tricks, including Roll Over, Dead Dog, and Crawl.

Dog Talk

Down means lie down on the floor or ground and hold still.

1. Have your dog on the leash, hold the leash in your left hand, and have a treat in your right hand.

2. Have your dog Sit by your left side and place your left hand (still holding the leash) on his shoulder.

3. Let your dog sniff the treat in your right hand. As he sniffs, take the treat (leading his nose) to the ground immediately in front of his toes as you tell him, "Fido, Down."

4. As his nose follows the treat in your hand, take the treat forward to give his body room to lie down. The left hand on his shoulder can apply slight pressure to encourage him to go down.

5. After your dog is Down, praise him and pop the treat in his mouth.

6. Let him hold the Down while he eats the treat and then release him.

7. Repeat for a total of five repetitions and give your dog a break. Repeat again later.

Bet You Didn't Know

Make an "L" signal with the treat; think "L" for "lie down." Start at the dog's nose, down to his paws, and then complete the base of the "L" by moving forward a few inches.

Troubleshooting

If your dog stands up to go to your hand with the treat, you're making too broad a gesture with the treat, or are moving your hand too quickly. Keep the hand signal slow and lead your dog by the nose.

After your dog is moving well into position, following your hand signal, after several days or even a week or more, begin making the signal without the treat. However, if your dog refuses, go back to the treats for several more training sessions. Eventually, you will want to use only the hand signal.

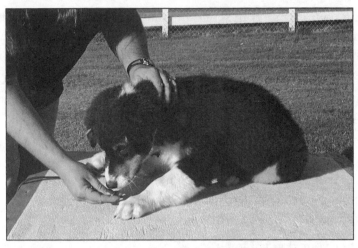

Use the lure to bring the dog's nose down toward his front paws and then forward, allowing his body to lie down. Praise and reward him.

Adding the Stay

The Down Stay is exactly like the Sit Stay except the dog is lying down. You will find the Down Stay easier to teach than the Sit Stay was initially. After all, the dog now already knows the Stay, and when he's lying down, he's more comfortable. It's easier for him to hold the Stay. But follow the training steps anyway. Even if your dog knows the Stay, this will help ensure his reliability.

1. With the leash on your dog, have some treats in your pocket.

2. Have your dog lie down; reward him with praise and a treat. Tell him "Stay" and make the Stay hand signal.

3. Don't step away yet, however; stand up next to your dog (rather than bend over him). Wait ten seconds.

4. Praise and reward your dog, and then release him.

5. Repeat for a total of five repetitions and give him a break.

6. On the next training session, repeat numbers 1 and 2, but take one step away from your dog. Wait ten seconds, and reward and release your dog.

7. Repeat for a total of five repetitions and give your dog a break.

BARK **Troubleshooting**

If your dog is having trouble holding the Down Stay, remain close to him (don't step away) and keep one hand on his shoulder. If he tries to get up, pressure on his shoulder from that hand can remind him to remain down.

The Down Stay is a command you will use in many different situations, so practice it often.

Very gradually increase the time and distance you ask your dog to hold the Down Stay, just as you did for the Sit Stay. Remember to increase one training criteria at a time (either the distance or the time or your position).

Making Eye Contact

The first thing I had you practice with your dog was getting his attention. You needed to do this simply so you could begin teaching him. Now that you have taught your dog a few exercises and you have some experience teaching him, we'll introduce the *Watch Me* command. The two exercises are much alike, but when we teach Watch Me, we'll introduce a command and we'll increase the distractions.

1. With your dog on a leash, hold the leash in your left hand and have a treat in your right hand.

Dog Talk

Watch Me means pay attention to me and ignore distractions.

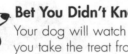

Bet You Didn't Know

Your dog will watch you take the treat from his nose to your face and might think you're going to eat it yourself! That's okay, he's going to watch what you're doing. Praise him as soon as he looks from the treat to your face. Watch his eyes move.

2. Have your dog Sit and reward him.

3. Let your dog sniff the treat in your right hand. Tell him, "Fido, Watch Me!" and take the treat from his nose to your chin.

4. His eyes will follow the treat. When his eyes move from the treat to your face, praise him, "Good boy!" and pop the treat in his mouth.

5. Repeat for a total of five repetitions and give him a break.

When your dog is watching you intently on command (usually after a week or more of training), begin making it more challenging.

1. Have your dog Sit in front of you, facing you, and do a Watch Me.

2. Take a step to your right side, asking your dog to watch you as you move. You might need to repeat the Watch Me command and hand signal to keep his attention.

3. Reward him when he does. Repeat for five repetitions each
    training session.

At your next training session, repeat the exercise while taking a
step to the left.

Over the next few training sessions, challenge your dog to watch
you while you move around. You can walk back and forth several
steps to the right and left, moving in front of your dog. You can also
back away from your dog, asking him to move with you while watching you. Keep your dog's excitement level high, praise often, and use
some good treats.

When your dog is focused on you, he can more
easily ignore distractions.

Continue using the treats as lures for this exercise for as long as
you need to use them. If your dog is easily distracted, use some
really good treats and vary them each training session. Make sure

your praise is good, too. This is a wonderful command, one that you will use with your obedience training as well as your trick training.

> **BARK** **Troubleshooting**
> Problems with Watch Me usually result from poor timing. As your dog's eyes flick to your face, praise him! The treat can arrive later; he understands that the praise marks his good behavior.

Walking with You

Most dog owners walk their dogs regularly; after all, that's one of the things most people enjoy about having a dog. However, many dogs don't walk nicely. They pull, dragging their owners, and dash from side to side across the sidewalk. This can cause neck and shoulder problems for the dog and wrist, arm, and shoulder problems for the owner. In addition, it really isn't much fun walking these dogs.

However, when a dog walks nicely on the leash without pulling, and walks calmly by the owner's side, going for a walk is much more pleasurable. Good walking skills are also needed for several tricks I'm going to introduce later.

1. Have your dog on his leash, hold the leash in your left hand, and have some treats in your right hand.

2. Have your dog Sit in front of you, facing you.

3. Ask your dog to watch you and when he does, back up a few paces, encouraging him to follow you.

4. After five paces or so (you really don't need to count), reward him with praise and a treat.

5. Repeat for a total of five repetitions and give him a break.

At your next training session, repeat the first four steps but back up a few more paces. Reward your dog.

When you know you can keep your dog's attention for those extra paces, you're ready to move on to the next training steps. If you don't have your dog's attention, don't move on.

6. Repeat the first four training steps, but instead of stopping to reward your dog, back up a few more paces and then turn as you're walking so that your dog ends up on your left side and you're walking forward together side by side. Praise and reward your dog lavishly.

7. Repeat for a total of five repetitions and quit for this training session.

At each subsequent training session for several days (even a couple of weeks), begin by backing away from your dog. This, with the Watch Me command, teaches him to focus on you while walking with you. It's like that old adage about chewing bubble gum and skipping rope at the same time—it's tough to do!

When your dog is doing well through these training steps, you're ready to move on. The next few steps will teach the *Heel* command.

Dog Talk
Heel means walk nicely by my left side without pulling.

1. Have your dog on leash, with the leash in your left hand and treats in your right hand.

2. Have your dog Sit by your left side, with his shoulder next to your left leg. Tell him, "Fido, Watch Me!"

3. When he's paying attention to you, step forward as you say, "Fido, Heel!"

4. As he steps forward with you, praise him, "Good boy!" If he gets distracted or begins to forge ahead, get his attention with the treat, letting him sniff it and repeating the Watch Me command.

5. After several paces, stop, praise, and reward your dog.

6. Repeat for a total of five repetitions and quit for a little while.

Keep training sessions short and sweet so that your dog has a chance to succeed. If you ask your dog to Watch you and Heel for a three-mile walk, he simply won't be able to do it. You'll both be frustrated and your training will suffer a setback. Instead, keep it short, sweet, and positive. Later, with practice, he'll be able to Heel for longer distances and times.

> **BARK Troubleshooting**
> If your dog dashes out in front of you, simply turn and go another direction. Let him discover you're not where you were. When he comes back to you, do a Watch Me and praise him. Repeat as often as needed.

Motivating the Come

The *Come* is a very important command, and one that could potentially save your dog's life someday. In addition, it can be a part of many other obedience exercises and tricks and is a vital part of other dog sports and activities.

> **Dog Talk**
> Come means your dog should go directly to you when you call him, without any detours, no matter what the distractions.

1. Have your dog on his leash, held in your left hand, while holding a treat in your right hand.

2. Let your dog have the length of his leash. Do not ask him to watch you; instead, let him get distracted by smells in the grass or other family members.

3. Back away from your dog as you call him, "Fido, Come!" in a happy tone of voice. Show him the treat as you call him.

4. If he's slow or distracted, you have the leash in one hand to encourage him to follow you. Do not yank him with the leash; just use gentle guidance to help him make the right decision.

5. When he begins moving toward you, praise him, "Good boy to Come!"

6. After taking a few steps backward, stop, and praise and reward him.

7. Do a total of five repetitions and stop for this session.

When your dog is coming to you on his own, with little resistance, repeat these training steps in an area where there are more distractions. If the neighborhood kids are playing outside, take your dog out and practice there. Or go to the local park. Make sure your dog understands that the Come applies everywhere, no matter what else is going on around him.

When he's doing well with distractions, use a long leash or a twenty-foot length of clothesline and repeat all the training steps above with this longer leash. This will teach your dog that even if he's farther away from you, he still needs to listen to the Come command.

Troubleshooting
Use a very happy tone of voice to call your dog to Come. Don't order him to Come with a drill instructor tone of voice; he will back away instead!

Down, Boy!
Do not take your dog off leash to practice the Come until he is mentally mature and very well trained. Unfortunately it's too easy for him to run away from you, and when he does, he learns he can.

Tips for Successful Training

Training is not always easy; it can be frustrating and repetitious, and it might proceed more slowly than you think it should. However, training can also be extremely rewarding. When you successfully teach your dog and that light bulb goes on over his head, "Hey! I get it!" all your efforts will be worthwhile. If you are patient with your dog, and keep your training positive and fun, you will also sense a deepening in the relationship you share.

Here are some tips for successful training:

- Keep that "fantastic five" in mind. Always do five repetitions of each new training step and then give your dog a break or move on to something else.

- During those breaks, which can be just a couple of minutes or a couple of hours, let your dog relax, sniff, go potty, or take a nap.

- Be patient with both yourself and your dog. This is a learning process for you both.

- Be consistent with your rules and your training. For example, if you ask your dog to Sit for his meals, do so all the time.

- Allow yourself to have fun. Training doesn't have to be like military boot camp; have fun with it!

The Least You Need to Know

- Teach the basic commands: Sit, Down, Stay, Release, Watch Me, Heel, and Come.

- The basic commands are the foundation for everything you will teach your dog in the future, including tricks.

- Follow the training steps; don't take shortcuts.

- Keep your training sessions upbeat and fun, but retain control.

Chapter **3**

Training the Intermediate Commands

In This Chapter

- 🏠 Moving beyond basic obedience
- 🏠 Teaching your dog to retrieve
- 🏠 Introducing off-leash skills
- 🏠 Working with distractions

The obedience exercises taught in Chapter 2 are the basics; everything you do with your dog begins there. Your trick training will be more successful if your dog understands those exercises and performs them reliably. After he knows them well, you can move on to the exercises presented here. These are intermediate obedience exercises that are not necessary for all dogs but are vital for many of the tricks presented in following chapters.

As with the basic commands, these exercises are introduced using a step-by-step method; don't skip ahead. Instead, work through the steps, repeating them as needed, so that your dog has a good understanding of the material before you move on. And remember, although some of this training has potentially serious consequences (such as off-leash control), keep the training fun.

Teaching the Stand

The *Stand* teaches your dog to stand still. Although this isn't nearly as important as the Sit, it is nice around the house. You can have your dog Stand while you towel him off after he's been out in the rain or at the grooming salon (he must Stand for bathing, brushing, and grooming), and it also has many applications for trick training.

Dog Talk

Stand means stand upright on all four paws and hold still.

The Stand is not difficult to teach.

1. Have your dog on a leash, Sitting by your left side. Hold the leash and a treat in your right hand. Your left hand should be empty and free.

2. Let your dog sniff the treat and tell him, "Fido, Stand," as you take one step forward, encouraging him to move from the Sit position.

3. As he steps forward, praise him, and place your left hand under his belly just in front of his back legs so you can keep him from Sitting and from continuing to walk forward.

BARK **Troubleshooting**

If your dog is confused with the Stand, don't worry. After all, you've taught him that Sitting is good! Just be patient, use your treats to lure him into position, and use your hands and voice to keep him there.

4. Your right hand can give him the treat as you praise him. If he tries to continue walking forward, your right hand can hold his collar in front of his chest to stop him.

5. When he's stood still for a few seconds, release him, praise him, and then repeat for a total of five repetitions.

The left hand under his belly and in front of his rear legs can stabilize your dog as you praise him.

When your dog is Standing easily without trying to Sit or walk forward, begin decreasing the use of your left hand. Just touch the front of his right rear leg as you tell him to Stand instead of putting your hand under his belly. With practice you should be able to use the lure in your right hand to bring him up and forward, without using the left hand at all.

When your dog will bring himself into the Stand position with a signal from your right hand and a verbal command, and without the use of your left hand, you can begin adding the Stay command. As your dog is Standing, simply tell him to Stay as you do with the Sit and Down commands. Let your dog hold it for a few seconds, praise him, and release him. You can gradually increase the time from a few seconds to ten to fifteen seconds.

You can also teach your dog to Stand from a moving Heel as well as from a Sit. Don't try to teach this until he knows the Stand from the Sit and is doing it well.

1. Have your dog on leash, Sitting in the Heel position by your left side. Hold the leash and a treat in your right hand and keep your left hand empty and free.

2. Tell your dog, "Fido, Watch Me!" When you have his attention, "Fido, Heel." Walk forward.

3. When he's walking nicely, tell him, "Fido, Stand," as you place your left hand in front of his right rear leg and right hand in front of his chest to stop forward movement. Praise him as he comes to a stop and Stands.

4. If he tries to Sit, the left hand at his right rear leg can slide under his belly, "Fido, Stand! Good!"

5. After he has stood for a few seconds, continue walking forward, "Fido, Heel! Good boy!" Praise him, give him the treat, and release him from the Heel.

You can make a great game out of the *Stand in Motion* by alternating sits and Stands from the Heel.

1. Begin Heeling with your dog, stop and have your dog Sit. Reward him.

2. Begin Heeling, stop and have your dog Stand. Reward him.

3. Begin Heeling, stop and have your dog Sit. Reward him.

When your dog can do both, depending on your command, mix them up instead of alternating them. Do three stops and Sits and then one Stand. Do three Stands and then one Sit. Heel at a jog (instead of a walk) and then ask him to Stand. Keep the training exercises active and stimulating, and encourage your dog to listen and think.

Dog Talk

Stand in Motion means stop moving forward and Stand still.

Perfecting the Retrieve

Many dogs are natural retrievers and will chase anything thrown, bringing it directly back so it can be thrown again. These dogs don't care if the thing being thrown is a tennis ball, a rope toy, or a stick; they simply love the game! Other dogs will chase the toy, maybe even pick it up, but get distracted and do not bring it back. Some dogs will watch their owners toss a ball or toy but have no desire to go get it, never mind bring it back.

Because there is so much canine variety regarding the retrieve, training it can be confusing. Should you go through all of the training steps when your dog already retrieves naturally? Or should you skip ahead? If your dog has no desire to retrieve on his own, should you even try to do this? I'm going to make your decision easy. Yes, train the retrieve. All dogs should be able to retrieve; it's great exercise for the dog and it's fun for both the dog and owner. It's also good training disguised as a game. So go through all the training steps even if your dog is a natural retriever or a nonretriever.

Bet You Didn't Know

You can use any command you wish for the retrieve; I use "Get It." You can use that, or "Fetch," or anything you wish. Just be consistent and use the same command when you teach it.

Playing Tug-of-War

Now you're going to teach your dog to play tug-of-war, a necessary step to learning the retrieve. To play this game you need a toy your dog can get excited about. The best toys for this are the knotted rope toys you can find at pet supply stores. They come in different sizes, so choose one that is small (or large) enough for your dog's mouth.

Tug-of-war has gotten a lot of bad press lately; some trainers feel it teaches the dog to be aggressive toward his owner. That's possibly true, but only if the dog wins every game. The important part of tug-of-war is who has the toy at the end of the game, and you're going to win every single time. But as you play, you're also going to make your dog really excited about this toy, and that can help immensely when we begin the retrieve.

1. Have your dog on leash so you can control the situation should he get overexcited.

2. Hold the rope toy in both hands, one hand at each end.

3. Offer it to your dog by shaking it in front of his nose. "What's this? Do you want it? Huh?"

4. When he makes a move toward it, even if he doesn't grab it, praise him. "Good boy! Yeah!"

5. When he grabs it, tell him, "Fido, Get It!" and shake it a little. Not too rough, but just enough to get him excited. Then praise him.

6. After a few shakes, tell him calmly (but not angrily), "Fido, Give."

7. If he takes his mouth off the toy, praise him enthusiastically. If he doesn't, pull a treat out of your pocket and offer it. He'll have to drop the toy to take the treat.

BARK Troubleshooting

If your dog will not drop the toy for a treat, with one hand reach over his muzzle and, with your fingers and thumb, press his top lips against his top teeth. When he pulls back, praise him, "Good boy to Give!"

8. When he understands *Give* means drop the toy, you can then call an end to the game any time you want. This is the important part of this game; when you win every time, you can make sure your dog doesn't take advantage of it.

After each play session, put the toy away where your dog can't get it. Keep it special for these times; if he has access to it all the time, it won't be nearly as special and exciting.

When your dog is bouncing around and begging to play when he sees this toy, you're ready to move on to the retrieve.

Teaching the Retrieve

If your dog is a natural retriever, you won't have any trouble teaching the retrieve. You just need to teach some commands to go along with the actions. You might also need to establish some control; some natural retrievers can be fanatics about their game. Just follow along with the steps and emphasize the verbal commands.

If your dog is not a natural retriever, it's important to keep the level of excitement high so he learns that this game is great fun. Watch your dog. When his enthusiasm dips, go back to a tug-of-war game and get him excited again. Make sure, too, you stick to the "fantastic five" repetitions; always stop the game leaving your dog wanting more. If you do too many retrieves, you might bore him, or get him so tired he loses enthusiasm.

1. Put your dog on leash so you can control him should he decide to dash away.

2. Have the rope toy in both hands (a hand at each end) and begin a tug-of-war game. When he grabs it, tell him, "Fido, Get It!" and praise him. Shake the toy and praise him.

3. Tell him to Give and take the toy from him. Praise him again.

4. Do this for a total of five repetitions and give him a short break.

5. When you come back from your break, offer the toy to your dog, play a quick game of tug-of-war, and then ask him to give it to you.

6. When he does, praise him and toss the toy to the ground in front of you two feet away. Tell your dog, "Fido, Get It!"

7. When he moves toward it, praise him. When he picks it up, praise him.

8. When he turns toward you to bring it back, tell him, "Fido, Bring It Here!" and praise him.

BARK **Troubleshooting**
If your dog tries to dash off with the toy, you have his leash. Guide him back to you and praise him.

9. When he brings it to you, play a quick game of tug-of-war. Ask him to give you the toy and praise him again.

10. Repeat for a total of five repetitions and take a break.

Over several days and several short training sessions, begin throwing the toy farther away. Don't start out tossing it fifty feet away; after all, you want to set your dog up to succeed, not learn bad habits like playing keep-away with the toy. Instead, toss it three feet away, then six, twelve, and fifteen feet. Always play this game in sets of five repetitions, with a break in between, and always stop the game before your dog becomes tired or bored.

The Retrieve can be great fun, is good exercise, and is a vital step in several tricks.

Introducing Other Toys

After your dog has decided that retrieving the rope toy is great fun, you should be able to introduce other toys with little difficulty.

When there is room on the toy for one of your hands and the dog's mouth, just play a little tug-of-war to get him excited and then begin some short tosses. When you use his known verbal commands (Get It, Bring It Back, and Give) he should fall into pattern with the new toy.

BARK) Troubleshooting _____

If your dog has trouble retrieving new toys, introduce one new toy at a time. Choose one that can be tugged or one that has a handle (such as a tennis ball on a rope) and go through the training steps for the tug-of-war and retrieve. When that toy is accepted as a good retrieving toy, add another one.

Training Off-Leash Skills

Teaching your dog to comply with you when he's off leash can be hard. Although some dogs make the transition easily, without seeming to notice that the leash is no longer attached to their collar, other dogs will take off for a long and potentially dangerous run.

To keep your dog safe, never attempt to train off leash without following the training steps outlined here. In addition, always be aware of where you are and what is surrounding you. Train inside with the outside doors closed or train outside in a securely fenced area. Make sure no one is going to open the door or gate and leave it open while your dog is off leash. Be aware and be safe.

 **Down, Boy!** _____

Do not attempt to do off-leash work with a puppy. Only mentally mature, well-trained dogs should be worked off leash.

Before starting any off-leash training, evaluate your dog.

🏠 How old is he? If he's less than eighteen months of age, give him some time to grow up. Although there are a few exceptions, most dogs under eighteen months of age are still mentally immature.

- Is he mentally mature? Some dogs are still mentally immature at two or even three years of age. If your dog has a hard time concentrating on anything (except maybe his dinner) and he is easily distracted, wait a while longer before beginning this training.

- How are his basic obedience skills? Your dog should know all the basic obedience exercises well and do them reliably. He should be able to perform all of them without lures, although food rewards are still fine.

- What breed (or mixtures of breeds) is your dog? Some breeds have a difficult time controlling themselves off leash. Many of the sighthounds, especially retired and rescued racing grey-hounds, should not be off leash outside of a fenced-in yard. If you have a breed (or an individual dog) that was bred to run, is known to be stubborn, or is particularly defiant, be cautious doing off-leash work.

If you feel you can safely begin off-leash training, find a place where you and your dog can be safe. A fenced-in yard with a secure gate is great.

1. Have your dog on leash, Sitting in the Heel position by your left side. Have some really good food treats in your pocket with a few in your right hand.

2. Tuck the leash into the left pocket of your pants, or if you don't have pockets, into the waistband of your pants. Maintain your left hand in its normal position as if you were still holding the leash.

3. Do a Watch Me with the treats in your right hand.

4. When you have your dog's attention, move forward, "Fido, Heel! Good boy!"

5. After several steps, stop and have your dog Sit. Praise him.

6. Do a total of five repetitions and give your dog a break or practice something else.

Repeat these training steps over a couple of weeks, gradually making the distance you walk longer. Then make the Heel itself more challenging. Walk a zigzag pattern, turn corners to the right and to the left, Heel in a figure eight pattern, and do quick about-turns. Heeling by itself can be boring, and although your dog needs this practice, nothing says you and he must both be bored by doing it.

When your dog is heeling nicely with you without pulling the leash out of your pocket, you're ready to move on.

> **Troubleshooting**
>
> If your dog has a hard time maintaining his attention on you while heeling, go back to the basic Watch Me and Heel exercises in Chapter 2. Repeat those training steps until your dog's skills are up to par for this training.

1. For the next few training sessions, have two leashes. Hook both up to your dog's collar. Tuck one in your left pocket (or waistband) and the other in your back pocket.

2. Sit your dog by your left side in the Heel position, do a Watch Me with a good treat in your hand, and walk forward, "Fido, Heel!"

3. Walk a few steps, stop, Sit your dog, and praise him.

4. Reach down and unhook the leash that's in your side pocket. Let it hang free so it's obvious to your dog it's unhooked. (The second leash is your safety leash; it's still tucked into a back pocket, hooked to your dog's collar.)

5. Repeat your Heel exercises, walking nicely at first, and as your dog shows he can do this, challenging him. Keep the treats good and the praise awesome.

After several training sessions over a couple of days or even a week, when your dog is walking without testing the leash, with no pulling, and is maintaining his attention on you, go back to using one leash.

1. Hook the leash to your dog and hold it in your left hand with the dog sitting nicely in the Heel position. Have some really good treats in your pocket and in your right hand.

2. Tell your dog, "Watch Me!" and "Fido, Heel!" and go for a walk. When you have his attention and he's working well, stop and Sit him, and praise him.

3. Unhook the leash and drape it around your neck. Tell him "Watch Me!" and "Fido, Heel!" and go for a walk.

4. When he's walking well, praise him. After a little walk, a short one to begin with, stop, Sit your dog, and give him a jackpot of praise.

5. Repeat for a total of five repetitions.

Now this doesn't mean your dog is completely trained for off-leash work; this is just the beginning. You should continue training in this manner for a while. Go back and forth between one leash, two leashes, and no leash. Use some really good treats and change them from training session to training session so they are always exciting.

You can use similar techniques for training the Stays and Comes off leash. Get a long leash (such as 30 feet of cotton clothesline rope). Hook that up to your dog's collar and practice Stays and Comes at a distance, using the long leash to make sure your dog doesn't decide to dash away. When you feel comfortable with your training, drop the long leash to the ground where you could step on it should you need it. Don't unhook the long leash from your dog's collar until you are 100 percent sure your dog will hold an off-leash Stay and will Come to you every time you call him.

Only mentally mature, well-trained dogs should work off leash.

Training with Distractions

All of your initial training should be done in a place where your dog is comfortable and secure. This might be your living room or the

backyard. When you teach your dog something new, you want as few *distractions* as possible because your dog needs to pay attention to you to learn.

Dog Talk

A **distraction** is something that gains your dog's attention so that he is no longer concentrating on you.

The learning process in dogs, however, is different than in people. When we learn something, we can make generalizations about it. For example, we were taught in school that two plus two equals four. And we know that two plus two equals four at home, in school, at work, and at the grocery store. Dogs, however, do not necessarily make the same generalizations. Your dog might learn that Sit means "lower your hips to the floor while keeping your front end up and hold still" while he's in the backyard. But he doesn't know that Sit has the same definition in different places unless he is taught in different places. After he's exposed to a variety of locations and distractions, and is required to sit in all of them, he might then learn that Sit is the same everywhere he goes.

Do not begin training with distractions until your dog is doing the obedience exercise or trick very well. When there is no confusion and your dog is repeating the exercise or trick reliably, then you might add a single distraction. What the distraction is depends on your individual dog. What is exciting to one dog might not be exciting to another. For example, my five-year-old Australian Shepherd, Riker, is not at all distracted by birds, but birds are a big distraction to my younger Aussie, Bashir. However, friendly people distract Riker and do not faze Bashir at all.

When you realize what distracts your dog, you can begin working with these things, one at a time. As you do, plan ahead and make sure you can set your dog up to succeed. Don't add so many distractions that your dog cannot succeed. Failures reproduce quickly and will hamper your training.

Here is an example of working with distractions during heeling. If your dog has been heeling nicely, you have probably cut back on many of the lure treats for the Watch Me. When adding distractions, you will use those treats again.

1. Have your dog on leash, sitting in the Heel position. Have some treats in your pocket and in your right hand. Make sure you have some really good treats that you know your dog likes.

2. Ask a friend or neighbor to sit on the grass nearby with a tennis ball. She can roll the ball, toss it from hand to hand, or bounce it.

3. Have your dog watch you, and when you have his attention, tell him, "Fido, Heel!" and walk a large circle around your friend.

4. When your dog looks at the tennis ball, show him the treat again and repeat the Watch Me command. When he looks back at you, praise him!

5. When he's focused on you and is ignoring the ball, stop, have him Sit, and praise him enthusiastically.

6. Repeat this exercise, making the circle smaller, reversing direction, and challenging your dog to pay attention to you. When he does well, praise and reward him. When he loses focus, bring him back with the Watch Me and praise.

7. Repeat for a total of five repetitions and take a break.

BARK) **Troubleshooting**

If you cannot get your dog's attention with the Watch Me command, ask your friend to stop moving the ball. Have your dog Sit with his back to the ball, and do a Watch Me. Bend over, move the hand with the treat, and work to get your dog's attention back on you. When his eyes move to you, praise him and pop the treat in his mouth right away. Don't ask him to Heel again until he's calm and focused.

Some common canine distractions include …

🏠 Other dogs, especially dogs in motion: running, playing, sniffing, or even other dogs training.

🏠 Other animals, including cats, rabbits, ferrets, and squirrels.

🏠 Food, both dog foods and human foods.

🏠 Moving objects, such as balls, Frisbees™, bicycles, and skateboards.

🏠 Children playing.

As you begin training with distractions, try to control when and where you encounter them, especially those that really stimulate your dog. For example, if kids running and playing are a big distraction, begin exposing your dog down the block from the local school. Your dog will know the kids are there and might hear them playing but won't be able to see them. Later, when he's no longer distracted there, you can move a little closer to the school. Later still, you might train in front of the school. Training with distractions makes your training stronger but only when your dog is able to succeed.

The Least You Need to Know

- The Stand is a very useful exercise by itself, but is also the beginning exercise for several tricks.

- Retrieving games are great fun, good exercise, and lead into both tricks and practical applications around the house.

- Dog owners are continually tempted to take the leash off their dogs, but only well-trained, mentally mature dogs should work off leash.

- Training with distractions can make your training stronger, but you need to control the distractions so your dog continues to succeed in his training.

Chapter **4**

Setting Realistic Goals

In This Chapter

- 🏠 Knowing your dog's abilities
- 🏠 Recognizing your dog's limitations
- 🏠 Setting short-range goals
- 🏠 Keeping an eye on long-range goals

All dogs are not created equal. Each individual dog has his or her own abilities and limitations. Some are more energetic and athletic; others enjoy lounging on the sofa. Most dogs thrive on a regular training routine and enjoy learning new things, but others have a hard time mastering the basics. Not only do these differences affect how your dog learns, but they can affect your relationship with your dog should you get angry, frustrated, or depressed over your dog's ability (or inability) to do what you ask him to do.

In this chapter we'll take a look at dogs in general and your dog specifically so you can set some realistic goals for training. I will also help you determine what you want to do with your trick training in the future so you can work toward that ultimate goal.

Understanding Your Dog's Abilities

Recently my dog training business, Kindred Spirits Dog Training, sponsored a trick-training class. We had twelve dogs and owners in the class. There was Molly, a beautiful white Standard Poodle; Chuck, a large Bloodhound-type mixed breed; Jasper and Lily, both Jack Russell Terriers; and several other talented dogs and owners, many already certified therapy dogs.

It was interesting to watch these dogs progress because the differences in their abilities was marked. Molly loved to jump and with some training was jumping through hoops, over a stick, over her owner's grandchildren, and through the grandchildren's arms. Chuck, on the other hand, wasn't nearly as cooperative, and although he did learn some tricks, he was more interested in sniffing the grass. Chuck wasn't dumb (nor was his owner a bad trainer), he just had other things on his mind and was difficult to motivate. Jasper and Lily were quick, athletic, and easy to teach, although they were also easily distracted.

Knowing your dog will help you immensely, not just with the training but also with setting goals. Molly's owner has quite a few different things she wishes to teach Molly, and knowing the two of them, I'm sure they will succeed. Chuck's owner just wants to teach him a few simple tricks so they can have fun together. Again, because she knows her dog well, I'm sure they, too, will succeed.

Knowing His Breed Heritage

Every dog breed in existence was designed for a particular purpose. Some breeds were guard dogs, several breeds protected domestic animals from predators, and others hunted vermin. Rottweilers herded cattle and pulled wagons; Border Collies herded sheep; Dachshunds hunted badgers. If there was a job to do, a dog did it.

By breeding dogs for specific jobs, several unique abilities and limitations were bred into them. The dogs bred to pull wagons are calm, steady, and strong. Those who herded sheep have good vision, and are quick and athletic. The characteristics bred into your dog have a great deal to do with how he will react to training and his ability to do what you ask him to do.

Your dog's size, physical conformation, and breed heritage should help you decide what tricks to attempt to train.

The dogs classified as herding dogs (which includes Border Collies, Australian Shepherds, both Corgis, and Shetland Sheepdogs) are quick learners, intelligent, and thrive when given something to do. These dogs are more apt to get into trouble when bored. Most take to trick training quickly and easily.

 Bet You Didn't Know

Australian Shepherds are not from Australia but instead were developed in the American west as all-purpose farm and ranch dogs. They enjoy participating in dog sports.

The working dogs include Rottweilers, Great Pyrenees, and Alaskan Malemutes. These dogs were all bred to perform a job; some of those jobs were very specific. Although most of these breeds are easily trained, some can also have a strong stubborn streak. Finding what motivates these dogs is the key to training them.

Bet You Didn't Know

Labrador Retrievers have been the most popular dog in the United States for several years. They have surpassed German Shepherds as the favorite breed for guide dog and service dog work.

The sporting dogs (which includes all of the retrievers and setters) were, for the most part, bred to run, swim, and retrieve birds for their hunting masters. These are energetic, active dogs with excellent scenting abilities. Most sporting dogs enjoy training, although they can also be easily distracted, especially when young.

The hounds are hunters. Scent hounds (such as the Beagles and Bassets) follow their nose, while sighthounds (Greyhounds and Salukis, for example) use their vision. Both types of hounds can be very single-minded; nothing matters except finding that prey. This can make training a challenge, but it's certainly not impossible; you just have to find the motivator that will keep your hound's attention.

Terriers (including the Cairn, Norfolk, and Norwich terriers) are also hunters—and fierce ones at that. Most were designed to hunt vermin (mice and rats) and so are fast, agile, and persistent. Terriers love training that is fun and not overly harsh; they take to trick training easily.

Bet You Didn't Know

Parson and Jack Russell Terriers are very popular, thanks, in part, to Eddie on the television show *Frasier*. These dogs are intelligent, active, and very busy!

Most of the toy breeds were bred to be companions. Although some, including Papillons, were also mousers, others were alarm watch dogs (they barked to warn of intruders but didn't bite). Most toys take to trick training quickly and enthusiastically. They love applause and enjoy the spotlight.

The breeds relegated to the American Kennel Club's Non-Sporting Group are quite different from each other. This group has become a catchall for breeds that didn't seem to fit into the other categories. This makes generalizations hard, as each of these breeds is quite unique. If your dog is a part of the non-sporting group, do some breed research to find out what the breed was originally designed to do; this will help you understand your dog a little better.

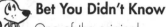

Bet You Didn't Know
One of the original occupations for the Bichon Frise was that of circus dog. These small fluffy white dogs performed a variety of tricks in small circuses that traveled through Europe.

Knowing your dog's breed can tell you a lot about him. If he is a herding, sporting, or hunting breed, he's going to like chasing things that move. The northern breeds are driven to run and pull. Terriers love to stick their noses in holes to find little critters. All of this knowledge can help you tailor a training program to your dog—and make your training more successful.

If you have a mixed-breed dog, breed research is a little harder. Sometimes you have to guess, depending on your dog's physical characteristics as well as his personal traits. Is he built like a Golden Retriever but is marked like a German Shepherd? Or does he look like a Beagle but has wiry hair like a terrier? Study your dog, and then study other dogs. What do you see? Although you might never know for sure what your mixed breed is, you can still help your training by understanding what tendencies his breed mixture might have and who he is as an individual.

Size Does Make a Difference

Size does make a difference in trick training, and you need to take it into account as you set your training goals. Although Molly, the Standard Poodle, is a tall dog, she is not heavy but is athletic and agile. So jumping through hoops and arms is easy for her. Although I'm sure the owner of a Newfoundland could teach his Newfie to perform the same tricks, it would not be nearly as easy, and the dog would have difficulty. Newfies are big, heavy-boned dogs bred to pull wagons and swim. Jumping is not important for their occupations. On the other hand, most toy-breed dogs excel in trick training. They might be small but most are quick and agile.

The same applies to body shape. A few years ago we had several Basset Hounds in one of our trick-training classes. Bassets are great clowns and love to wear costumes. One in particular, Gracie, always came to class wearing hats and feather boas, and they suited her perfectly. Gracie, however, was not at all athletic. She did not jump through hoops, weave through her owner's legs, or jump and weave through raised hoops. However, she did a great bow, said her prayers on command, and rolled over to bare her belly quite well.

Down, Boy!
Never ask your dog to perform a trick that could cause him harm. Keep your dog safe.

As you decide which tricks to teach your dog, take into account his size and body type. Choose tricks your dog can do safely and comfortably; do not ask him to perform any tricks that could cause him to hurt himself.

Appreciating His Personality

Gracie, the Basset, loved applause. Whenever she performed a trick in front of the class, she would wait for the laughter and applause before going on to another trick. But not all dogs love the spotlight; some have stage fright. So it's important to recognize your dog for who he is and not to force him into situations that will be uncomfortable for him.

Your dog's personality will also affect how you train him. Bright, intelligent, compliant dogs will move through the training steps much more quickly than dogs who might not be as bright, are more difficult to motivate, or are easily distracted.

One goal of all your training, including teaching tricks, should be to have fun with your dog. So relax and enjoy the time you're spending with him.

Setting Trick-Training Goals

You should be setting two different types of goals. *Long-range goals* are those things you would like to eventually accomplish. Those might include:

- Putting together a trick routine for future therapy dog visits.

- Designing a trick routine and costumes for an upcoming community canine trick-training contest.

- Developing a number of different tricks that you and your dog can have fun performing for your own amusement.

- Doing trick training as a fun intermission between obedience training sessions.

- Using trick training as a means to deepen the relationship with your dog.

Long-range goals can be posted on your calendar or daily planner in a spot where you will see them often. Each time you see this goal, it will help keep you thinking about it.

Dog Talk

Short-range goals are training steps; a daily goal might be one, two, or even three training steps. Long-range goals are tricks or commands you are working toward that will take some time and effort to accomplish.

Short-range goals are much more immediate and might be individual training steps. For example, you might decide that a reasonable goal today would be to have your dog sit on command the first time you ask and to hold it for ten seconds. Your goal tomorrow might be to have him sit for fifteen seconds.

If you try to remember what you're doing, and how your dog responds, from training session to training session, you will make mistakes. Our memories are notoriously flawed and we have a tendency to remember what we want to remember.

To avoid problems, you need to keep track of your training progress and your goals. You can use a diary or a journal, or even make notes in your daily planner. Consider a format such as this:

Date and time of training session: _____

Exercise or trick being taught: _____

First training step attempted today: _____

How many repetitions? _____

How did the dog respond? _____

How did I change the training to suit that response?

_____

Keep notes for each training step as you teach it. You can then review your notes later to make sure you're heading in the right direction. Or you can make adjustments should you get distracted or confused.

Teaching a therapy dog to do tricks or perform services is a wonderful long-range goal.

You can also make notes as to the types of treats or other positive reinforcements used during each training session. You can then go back and see if any specific reinforcements continually worked better (or worse) than others.

The Least You Need to Know

- Take your dog's abilities, size, body type, and breed heritage into consideration as you plan your trick training.

- Never ask your dog to do anything that could cause him to hurt himself; keep him safe.

- Establish some long-range goals so you know where your training is taking you.

- Short-range goals can help keep you focused.

Part  Building-Block Tricks

The first trick many people teach their dog is to Shake hands (or paws). This can easily be transformed into a Wave. Another easy trick is Wag Your Tail. Most happy dogs wag their tails, so why not turn it into a trick? That is, of course, if your dog has a tail. My breed of choice is Australian Shepherds, so my dogs do Wiggle Butt!

As you read through this section and begin training your dog to do a few of the tricks, make sure you keep your training fun. Be ready to laugh at yourself (you'll make mistakes as you go along, and that's okay) and laugh with (but not at) your dog.

Beginning with Some Easy Tricks

In This Chapter

- Learning how to teach a trick
- Starting with some simple tricks
- Teaching the Sit Pretty, Shake, Wave, and more
- Using a known trick to teach another

Many dog owners feel there is a secret to teaching dogs tricks; that a mysterious society of dog trainers knows something special and is keeping that knowledge from everyone else. Well, guess what? I'm going to share that knowledge with you!

Trick training is easy! All you need to do is remember the information passed along to you in the first four chapters of this book (refer back to that information to refresh your memory) and then follow along with the training steps laid out for you. If you run into a problem, check the "Troubleshooting" boxes. That's it! So go have some fun with these easy tricks.

> **Bet You Didn't Know** _____
> Your dog will be on leash for all the tricks taught in this chapter so you can keep him close, keep him from backing away from you during the training process, and so you can help him should he need some help. So even though the leash might not seem to be an essential part of the trick, keep it attached to your dog's collar.

Sit Pretty

This trick teaches your dog to sit up, balancing on his hips and tail, and hold still. *Sit pretty* is a great trick for first-time trick trainers because for most dogs, it's easy to do. It's a great trick for therapy dogs because it's eye-catching and amusing.

The only equipment you need for this trick is your dog's leash and some really good treats. Your dog should be able to Sit on command and hold that Sit until you release him.

> **Dog Talk** _____
> **Sit Pretty** means sit up, balance on your hips and tail, and hold still.

1. Have the leash on your dog; hold it in one hand and have a treat in your other.

2. Have your dog Sit in front of you and praise him for sitting.

3. Let your dog smell the treat in your hand and slowly lift the treat up from his nose.

4. As he begins to lift his body up to follow the treat, tell him, "Fido, Sit Pretty! Good!" and pop the treat in his mouth. Make sure he gets the positive reinforcements only when his front paws are off the ground.

5. Repeat for a total of five repetitions.

At your next training session, repeat the first four training steps.

For your next five repetitions, withhold the reward until he lifts his body slightly higher. Then pop the treat in his mouth as you praise him.

Your goal is to have your dog sit up completely, with his back straight, and his tail out behind him as a brace. (Tailless dogs are obviously at a slight disadvantage!)

When your dog can sit up completely, begin telling him, "Fido, Stay," and let him hold it for five seconds before you praise and release him. Very gradually, with time and practice, as his back muscles strengthen, he can hold the position for longer periods of time, but never have him do so for more than a minute each repetition.

BARK Troubleshooting
If your dog has trouble balancing, practice this with him backed into a corner. The wall on each side can help him maintain his balance.

BARK Troubleshooting
If your dog stands up on his back feet instead of lifting his body, you're lifting the treat from his nose too fast and too far. Keep the treat right in front of his nose (as if it's glued to his nose) and lure him up off his front paws.

Extending a Paw to Shake

This trick consists of teaching your dog to offer a paw so that you (or someone else) can *Shake* hands with him. The only equipment needed is your dog's leash and some good treats.

1. With your dog on leash, hold the leash in your left hand along with some treats. Have your right hand empty.

2. Depending on the size of your dog, bend over, sit, or kneel in front of him. You need to be able to reach his paw.

3. With your right hand, reach his right paw, and with one finger, tickle the hollow behind his paw (most dogs are ticklish there).

Dog Talk
Shake means lift your right paw toward me so we can touch hand to paw.

Troubleshooting
Some dogs are not ticklish and will not lift their paw when you try to tickle it. For these dogs, lift the paw in steps 3 and 4 of this trick.

4. As he lifts his paw slightly, tell him, "Fido, Shake!" Touch his paw with your hand, and praise and reward him.

5. Repeat for a total of five times.

At your next training session, repeat all five steps.

Your goal is to teach your dog to lift his paw toward your hand when he hears "Fido, Shake," so watch for him to begin lifting his paw toward your hand as you reach toward him. When he does, offer him a jackpot reward: more treats, enthusiastic praise, and some petting. At each subsequent training session, withhold the rewards for a second or two until he is reaching toward your hand a little more each time.

The Shake is a fun, easy trick that can also lead to Other Paw and Wave.

Offering the Other Paw

When your dog will shake hands (and paws!) well each time you ask, reaching that paw out toward your hand, you can then teach him to offer the *Other Paw*. When alternated with the shake trick, this makes your dog look very smart. People will be amazed that he knows the difference!

You will train this trick exactly as you did Shake, except reverse hands and paws. You will reach with your left hand toward your dog's left paw. Follow the same training steps; most dogs pick this up very quickly. As you train this trick, do not train Shake at the same time; you will confuse your dog. Instead, drop the Shake while training the Other Paw.

When your dog knows Other Paw well and will do it on command, then you can bring back Shake. Challenge your dog to listen and respond correctly. Ask him to Shake, then Other Paw, then Shake again. Reward each correct response. Then do three Shakes and two Other Paws, and then at another training session, four Other Paws and one Shake. Make a big fuss over him when he can follow your commands and do five repetitions correctly. "Yeah! Super Dog!"

Dog Talk

Whereas *Shake* means offer me your right paw, **Other Paw** means offer me your left paw.

Troubleshooting

If your dog tries to lift his right paw to your left hand, pull your hand back; do not shake his paw. When his paws are back on the ground, repeat the training step to his left paw.

Waving at Adoring Fans

The *Wave* is a great trick for showing off. Therapy dogs can wave good-bye at the people they have visited and you can ask your dog to wave at guests leaving your house. It's also a fun trick to combine with other tricks as part of a routine.

For this trick your dog must be able to Sit on command and hold still, and Shake paws on command. The only equipment you need are a leash and some good treats.

Dog Talk
Wave means lift your paw as high as your shoulder and move it up and down as if waving.

1. With your dog on leash, hold the leash in your left hand as well as some treats. Have your right hand empty.

2. Have your dog sit in front of you. Reach toward his paw as you tell him, "Fido, Shake."

3. As his paw moves toward your hand, pull your hand back so his paw just touches the tips of your fingers, and at the same time tell him, "Fido, Wave!" Praise and reward him.

4. Repeat for a total of five repetitions.

At your next training session, repeat the four steps for five repetitions. Begin emphasizing, "Fido, Wave" rather than Shake. "Fido, Shake. WAVE! Shake."

If your dog is reaching well toward your hand, begin lifting your hand higher so he has to reach higher than he did for the Shake. Continue having him just brush the tips of your fingers. Stop saying Shake and tell him only, "Fido, Wave!"

Bet You Didn't Know
As you're teaching this trick, make sure your dog is praised and rewarded when his paw is in the air. If you reward him late, he might think he's being rewarded for putting his paw back on the ground rather than waving it in the air.

Repeat these training steps for five repetitions each for two to three training sessions.

When your dog is reaching well, begin pulling your hand back completely when he is reaching up. Praise him enthusiastically when he completes the Wave without touching your hand.

Wag Your Tail

Your dog probably wags his tail naturally when he's happy. You can take advantage of this by giving the action a name and then trying to teach him an association between the command "*Wag Your Tail!*" and the natural action. Dogs without tails, like Australian Shepherds and Rottweilers, can wiggle their stub or their entire rear ends.

You need your dog's leash for this exercise, a favorite toy or ball, and some treats.

Dog Talk _____

Wag Your Tail means exactly that; wag your tail on command.

1. With your dog on leash, have him stand in front of you, either on command (asking him to stand) or by allowing him to stand naturally.

2. Hold the leash in one hand with some treats and have the ball or toy in your other hand.

3. Toss the ball or toy in the air to get your dog's attention. Tease him a little; say "Do you want the toy?" using a high-pitched, happy tone of voice.

4. When his tail wags, tell him, "Fido, Wag Your Tail! Good boy!" and toss him the toy or ball.

5. Let him play with it a moment and ask him to give it back to you. When he does, give him a treat.

6. Repeat for a total of five repetitions.

This trick will take many repetitions before your dog figures out what he's doing that you like. Tail wagging isn't a conscious movement; it just happens!

A dog will wag his tail naturally. The hardest part of this trick is to make him conscious of it.

Crawling for Applause

The *Crawl* is an easy trick for most dogs to learn and is a great one to combine with a costume or as a part of a trick routine. There are no size limits on this trick; big dogs and little dogs can do this equally well.

For equipment, you need your dog's leash, some good treats, and a low table (such as a coffee table) or a bench (like a picnic table bench). Place the table or bench in an area where you and your dog have room to move around it. Make sure nothing is on it just in case your dog stands up underneath it and tips it over.

Dog Talk

The definition of the **Crawl** is lay down on the floor or ground and move forward without getting up.

1. Have the leash on your dog and hold it in your left hand. Have some treats in your pocket and a few in your right hand.

2. Sit your dog in front of the table and then touch the table, rocking it a little so your dog notices it and is not worried about it.

3. Then have your dog lie down with his head close to the table.

4. From the same side of the table the dog is on, tell him, "Fido, Crawl" and reach under the table with your right hand (treat in the hand) so you can guide him under the table. If the table is low enough, it can keep him from standing up.

5. When he comes out from under the table at any point (where he went in, to one side, or all the way under to the other side), praise him, "Yeah! Awesome job!" and reward him.

6. Do a total of five repetitions, and then give your dog a break.

Repeat the first six steps during your next several training sessions.

When your dog will crawl nicely, without hesitation, move on to the next step.

7. Have your dog lie down on one side of the table and leave him, going to the opposite side. Kneel down so you can see him.

8. Tell him, "Fido, Come! Crawl!" and show him the treat.

9. When he begins crawling, praise him, and when he comes out the other side, give him a jackpot of praise and treats.

10. Repeat for a total of five repetitions.

Troubleshooting

BARK

If your dog is worried about the table, have him lie down and instead of having him crawl under something, simply place your left hand on his shoulder to keep him from popping up. Use the left hand and treat to lure him forward.

As your dog learns Crawl, you can stop using the Come command, and emphasize the Crawl command alone.

When teaching the Crawl with the hand on the dog's shoulder, keep the hand with the treat right in front of the dog's nose.

Move the treat forward so your dog tries to follow it. The hand on the shoulder keeps him from getting up.

When the dog understands the Crawl and won't pop up, the hand with the treat can become more of a hand signal and less of a lure.

Rolling Over (and Rolling Some More)

Rolling Over is easy and a commonly taught trick. But you can make it special by teaching your dog to *Roll Over* more than once, on command, and in the direction you indicate.

The only equipment you need for this trick is your dog's leash and some treats.

Dog Talk _____
Roll Over means lie down and roll your entire body over.

1. With your dog on leash, have him lie down, and then kneel or sit next to him. Have some treats in your right hand, along with the leash.

2. Put your left hand on your dog's shoulder.

3. Your right hand will show your dog the treat, and then make a big circle so you lead your dog's head. Keep the dog's nose following the treat.

4. As your dog leans to follow the treat, use your hand on the dog's shoulder to gently push him over as you tell him, "Fido, Roll Over!" Praise him as he rolls.

5. As he comes back to his starting position, pop the treat in his mouth.

6. Do not let him get up; keep him in the down position.

7. Repeat for a total of five repetitions and then take a break.

Repeat these training steps over the next several training sessions. When your dog is moving on his own and beginning to Roll Over under his own power, even if you have to help him a little, you're ready to move on.

Eventually the hand signal for the Roll Over will be a small circle sketched with your hand, moving in the direction you want your dog to roll. Therefore, as your dog begins to move well on his own, begin making the signal smaller but do so gradually. Instead of making a big circle bringing your dog's head around, make the circle from your dog's nose in the direction you want him to move, but decrease its motion over the dog's back. Over many training sessions over a few weeks, keep decreasing the signal until it's a small circle sketched in the air in front of your dog.

Troubleshooting

Some dogs feel vulnerable when rolling over and are hesitant to attempt this trick. For these dogs, teach it in even smaller steps than previously outlined, asking him to lie on his side first, then his back, then the other side. Praise and reward each small step, working to build some motivation so the dog wants to do this.

When your dog knows the signal, you can then add multiple Roll Overs. Simply sketch one circle, praise your dog after he's completed the Roll Over, and then ask him to do it again. When you first start this, you must reward each completed Roll Over, but when your dog is offering it eagerly, you can begin adding another one immediately following the completion of the first. When he does it well, give him a jackpot of positive reinforcements!

Use the treat as a lure to bring the dog's head around so the body follows.

Rolling Back

When your dog is rolling in one direction well (with that direction labeled as Roll Over) you can then teach your dog to roll in the other direction, or Roll Back!

Use exactly the same training steps outlined previously, except that you will be having the dog roll the other direction, so your hand signal will move to the opposite direction and the command will be "Fido, Roll Back." While you're training this trick, stop training Roll Over. Doing both at this point in training will be confusing.

However, after your dog knows Roll Back as well as he does Roll Over, you can alternate them. Ask him to Roll Over, then Roll Back.

Dog Talk

If *Roll Over* means for the dog to roll to his right, then **Roll Back** means roll to the left.

After your dog knows Roll Over, you can teach him to Roll Back by helping him roll the other direction.

Show Me Your Tummy!

This is another natural act that many dogs do daily; they roll onto their back so you can rub their tummy. You can always add the command *Show Me Your Tummy* when your dog rolls over on his own, but you can also teach it as a trick. As a trick, your dog needs to know Roll Over first.

Dog Talk

Show Me Your Tummy means roll over on your back, displaying your belly, and hold still.

1. With your dog on leash, kneel or sit next to your dog. Have a treat in one hand.

2. Ask your dog to roll over but have your hand ready to stop him as soon as he's on his back.

3. When you stop him, immediately praise him, "Show Me Your Tummy! Good boy!" and pop a treat in his mouth while he's still on his back.

4. Tell your dog to stay and gently rub his tummy.

5. After a few seconds, release your dog and praise him again, "Good boy!"

6. Repeat for a total of five repetitions and give your dog a break.

At your next training session, repeat these training steps until your dog is stopping on his back without your assistance. When he does stop on his own, give him a jackpot of positive reinforcements.

Go to Sleep

Go To Sleep (or Dead Dog if you prefer that) is a fun trick that simply requires the dog to be still. Of course, for some dogs that alone can be tough!

The only props you need to teach this command are your leash and some treats. After your dog knows it, this is a cute one to add additional props to, such as a pillow or even a blanket. It's a nice touch when you tell your dog "Fido, Go To Sleep," as you fluff up his pillow and then when he's down, cover him up with a nice comforter.

Dog Talk

Go To Sleep means lie down on your side with your head down and hold still.

1. With your dog on leash, have him lie down. Kneel down next to him.

2. Most dogs lie down with one back leg tucked up underneath. It's easier for them to roll to that side. So look at your dog so you can tell which way to have him move.

3. With one hand on your dog's hips and one on his shoulders, tell him, "Go To Sleep" and roll him onto his side. Praise him and pop a treat in his mouth while you help him hold that position for a few seconds. Release him and reward him.

4. Repeat for a total of five repetitions and take a break.

Repeat the training steps for the next couple of training sessions. When your dog is beginning to move onto his side on his own, you're ready to go on to the next training steps.

As you tell your dog to go to sleep, decrease the physical assistance you're offering (perhaps just use one hand on his shoulders). After he has rolled onto his side, praise and reward him, and then with one hand gently push his head down to the floor so he's flat on his side. Praise him, tell him to stay, and after a few seconds release him.

If you're using the command Dead Dog instead of Go To Sleep, you can teach your dog to listen to the command and pick it out of a conversation. I taught a German Shepherd to listen carefully (I did a finger flick toward him to cue Watch Me) and then would ask him, "Would you rather be (a policeman, nurse, teacher, or whomever I was talking to) or a Dead Dog?" He would drop to the ground, go flat on his side, with his head down and usually with his tail wagging furiously! The person I was talking to would gasp, think they were insulted, and then laugh at the great joke. Of course, part of the joke was the wagging tail!

Paws Up!

Paws Up is a great trick for therapy dogs; with this trick the dog can place his paws on bed rails so someone can more easily pet him. Or

he can put his paws on the arm of a wheelchair or the bar of a walker. Paws Up is also the first step in another trick, Say Your Prayers, that will be taught later.

To begin this trick, you need a chair with arms on it, your dog's leash, and some treats or a toy your dog really likes.

1. Sit in the chair, and with your dog on a leash, bring him close to one side of the chair, facing you (not parallel to you).

2. Show your dog the treat and pat the arm of the chair, encouraging him to bring his front paws up.

3. When he does, tell him, "Fido, Paws Up! Good boy!" and pop a treat in his mouth. Make sure his paws are still up when you praise him.

4. Tell him Stay, and help him hold it for just a few seconds.

5. Release him, praise him, and let him take his paws off the chair, placing them back on the floor.

6. Repeat for a total of five repetitions and take a break.

When your dog is doing this well, stand next to him as you ask him to lift his paws to the arm of the chair, following the same training steps outlined previously. When he can do that, try him on the bar of a walker, the arm of a wheelchair, and a variety of other horizontal bars. Just make sure you brace the item he's putting his paws on; and if your dog is on a slippery floor, brace him, too, so he doesn't slip and fall.

> **BARK Troubleshooting**
>
> If your dog is reluctant to lift his paws on his own, increase the excitement. Pat your chest, use a happy tone of voice, and then reward any small movement upward. When his paws finally come up, give him a jackpot reward!

Keeping It Fun!

This chapter taught eleven easy tricks, most based on a basic command, with some of the tricks related to each other. By teaching these commands, you can learn how to teach your individual dog and hopefully you've successfully taught several of them.

Just remember, keep your trick-training fun. Don't take it seriously, even if you're having trouble with a training step or a particular trick. Just back up a few steps and begin again. And then laugh. Laugh at yourself and laugh with your dog. After all, this is trick training and it's supposed to be fun!

The Least You Need to Know

- All of these tricks begin with the basic obedience commands, so be sure to review and practice those often.

- Your training skills (the tone of your voice, use of positive reinforcements, and using treats as lures) are all important to trick training.

- These easy tricks can be taught to most dogs; just do so carefully and protect your dog from hurting himself.

- Don't take your trick training seriously; this is fun!

Chapter 6

Tricks for the Busy Dog

In This Chapter

- 🏠 Teaching your dog Bow and Say Your Prayers
- 🏠 Spinning and dancing are great fun
- 🏠 Jumping safely
- 🏠 Jumping here and jumping there

Busy dogs need busy tricks that will engage not only their bodies but also their minds. When the dog's body and mind are both challenged, he's less apt to get into trouble, and that's always a good thing!

The tricks in this chapter begin with a couple of easy ones: the Bow and Say Your Prayers are not difficult. Then we'll move on to two active tricks: Spin and Dance. Both of these are wonderful for busy dogs. Then we'll really get moving with several different ways to incorporate jumping into tricks and trick routines.

A word of warning, however. Most of these tricks are best done off leash, so before you begin, make sure you review your dog's obedience skills, especially the Watch Me and the off-leash Come. Don't attempt these tricks in a place where your dog could dash away and come to harm. Instead, keep safety in mind and train them inside or in a fenced-in yard.

Bowing to the Crowd

The *Bow* is a very attractive trick, especially if your dog's tail is wagging happily and he has a big smile on his face. When the dog's audience applauds, it's quite a show-stopping trick.

Dog Talk

Bow means lower your front end to the ground, keeping your hips elevated, and wait for a release to end the trick.

Your dog will need to know the Stand command for this trick (see Chapter 3). The only equipment you need are some treats. If you have a small dog, however, you might want to teach this on a table or bench.

1. Kneel or sit on the floor and have your dog Stand in front of you, with his right side facing you, his head by your right hand and hips to your left.

2. Let your dog sniff the treat in your right hand.

3. Tell him, "Fido, Take a Bow!" and bring the treat down to his front paws.

4. As his head follows the treat, praise the downward movement.

5. Your left hand should be close to your dog's tummy, close to his back legs. If he begins to lie down, use that hand to keep his back end up.

6. After giving the treat, wait a second or two and then release him.

7. Repeat for a total of five repetitions.

Your eventual goal is to have the elbows of your dog's front legs on the ground, but in the initial training, praise and reward any downward movement of the front end. As he gets the idea, though, wait to reward him until the elbows are on the ground.

When Bowing, your dog's elbows should be on the ground while his hips remain high.

The Bow is a very natural behavior for dogs; it's a solicitation for play. You can see this by bowing to your dog. Lift both hands high in the air, and then give a little hop and bring them down in front of you, all the way to your knees, or if you're limber, all the way to the floor. Move your hips from side to side. Repeat it and then watch your dog's reaction. If you've done a good Bow impression, he will Bow back to you, bark, and bounce up and down. You've established communication! Now go play.

BARK **Troubleshooting**

If your dog insists on lying down (instead of keeping the back end up) you can loop a leash under his belly and use that as a sling to help keep his hips elevated.

Say Your Prayers

Say Your Prayers is a good trick to incorporate into a trick routine, plus it's a good trick for families with children who say their prayers each night. Fido can say his prayers right alongside the kids.

Your dog will need to know the Paws Up trick taught in Chapter 5 before beginning this trick. Train and practice Paws Up until your dog can do it well on a variety of chairs or the edge of the bed (use a sturdy lawnchair if you've taught him to stay off indoor furniture). The only equipment you will need is a chair with an arm or the side of a bed, and some treats.

Dog Talk

Say Your Prayers means lift your front paws to the surface indicated, and then lower your head to your paws and hold still until released.

1. Sit in a chair with an arm on it that you can have your dog do a Paws Up on. Have your dog approach the chair from the side. Have some treats in hand.

2. Tell your dog, "Fido, Paws Up" and encourage him to bring his paws up on the arm of the chair. Praise and reward him and tell him, "Fido, Stay."

3. Take a treat and let him sniff it. Lower the treat so his head moves down toward his paws on the arm of the chair.

4. As his head moves down, tell him, "Fido, Say Your Prayers!"

5. Praise the downward movement and pop a treat in his mouth when his head touches his front paws.

6. Repeat for a total of five repetitions.

When your dog is doing this easily and moving his head all the way down to his front paws, begin delaying the praise and treats for a few seconds so that he holds his head still for a few moments. Then praise, reward, and release him. You can also use the Stay command when his head is down. Just don't ask him to hold still more than a few seconds.

If your dog cannot stand on his back legs for any period of time (those with arthritis, or hip or back problems), you can teach this trick in a different format.

1. Sit or kneel on the floor and invite your dog to lie down in front of you (with his side to you).

2. Let your dog sniff a treat in your hand.

3. Take the treat to the floor for your dog, moving your hand slowly so he follows the treat to the floor.

4. When his head is down, hold the treat in your hand a moment as you tell him, "Fido, Say Your Prayers!"

5. Praise and reward him, then release him.

6. Repeat for a total of five repetitions.

Over several training sessions, gradually withhold praise and treats for a few seconds so your dog holds the position longer.

Spinning and Spinning!

Spin is a fast, exciting trick that many dogs absolutely love to do. It consists of teaching your dog to spin in a circle in front of you, and although you will begin with one circle (one Spin), as soon as your dog can do it you will add more Spins. Spin does not mean make your dog Spin until he throws up, though!

Dog Talk

Spin means turn in a circle, a small circle, right in front of me.

Practice the stand command a few times before you begin this trick. If your dog tries to do it from a sit, it won't work, so the stand is important. The only equipment you need for this trick is some really good treats.

1. With your dog standing in front of you, reach down so he can smell a treat in your hand.

2. Using the treat as a lure, begin moving your hand in a circle (moving either direction) so that he is following your hand and walking in a circle.

3. As he's moving, tell him, "Fido, Spin!"

4. After one circle, stop your hand, let him catch up and eat the treat, and praise him.

5. Repeat for a total of five repetitions.

Over several training sessions, gradually make the circles faster so the movement is more like a Spin and less like a walk. When your dog is moving quickly and completing the circle well, you can begin decreasing your hand signal. Eventually, you should be able to sketch a circle in the air as you tell your dog, "Fido, Spin!" But that takes time, so use the big signal as long as you need to.

If one dog spinning is good, two in unison is great!

BARK Troubleshooting
If your dog does not follow your hand in a circle, put the leash on him and hold it in the same hand as the treat. Lead the dog through the circle and follow the preceding training steps.

When your dog is circling well, with some good speed, and you've been able to decrease your hand signal a little, begin asking the dog to Spin more than once for a treat by repeating the hand signal and verbal command as the dog completes each circle. Keep the number of Spins random (sometimes twice, sometimes three times, sometimes once around) so your dog never really knows when he's going to get the treat. This randomness makes the circle faster and stronger.

Troubleshooting

BARK If your dog is having trouble moving in a circle, he's hesitant and slow, ask him to circle the other direction. Some dogs move more easily to the left, while others circle to the right more readily. It's just a personal thing, like being right-handed or left-handed.

Dancing Dog

This is an active trick for strong, healthy dogs who like to move. Although dogs of all sizes can do this trick, *Dance* is not for dogs with hip or back problems, dogs with arthritis, or heavy-bodied dogs. There are plenty of other tricks those dogs can do, so leave this one to the lighter-bodied, athletic dogs.

Dog Talk

Dance means stand on your back legs and dance.

The only props you need for this trick are some treats, but because this trick is hard, make sure you have some really good treats and vary those treats from training session to training session so they are always exciting.

Down, Boy!

Dance is a demanding, physically difficult trick. Do not ask dogs with back or hip problems, or dogs with arthritis, to do this trick.

Review the Stand before beginning this trick as your dog will start the trick from the Stand, not the Sit.

1. With your dog standing in front of you, let him sniff the treat.

2. Take the treat over your dog's head. He may look at it, sniff upward, and maybe even jump for it. Ignore those behaviors.

3. When he stands up on his back legs, tell him, "Fido, Dance!" Praise him and pop the treat in his mouth. (Make sure he gets the treat when he's up on his back legs, not when his front legs are back on the floor. You may have to toss it.)

4. Repeat for a total of five repetitions.

Repeat these steps over several training sessions.

After several days and several training sessions, when he is coming up easily for the treat and seems to understand the command, back away one step so that he hops for the treat. Only ask him to make one hop. Praise and reward him.

Troubleshooting Some dogs are worried about standing upright. If your dog appears concerned, switch treats and use something really good that he loves, like hot dogs! Hold the treats closer to his nose and get him concentrating on the treats. He'll stand tall!

Your goal is to have your dog stand upright and make a few hops so that he appears to be dancing. Those hops can be forward toward you, or if you move around, the hops can be following you. Ask for more hops very, very gradually over several weeks of training. You want to build your dog's back and hip muscles so he can do this without hurting himself.

Jumping Safely

The next few tricks in this chapter all require your dog to jump. Although almost all dogs can jump (other than those with physical disabilities), it is important that they also jump safely. It's too easy for a dog to hurt himself jumping, especially in the enthusiasm of learning some new tricks.

When introducing both jumping and new tricks, keep the jump heights low. Ankle height is great in the beginning. After all, the emphasis is on the new tricks, not the height of the jumps. Repeated low jumps will help your dog build muscle tone, especially if he hasn't done much jumping recently. Later, after weeks of low jumps, you can gradually increase the height of the jumps, but in most cases there is no need for the dog to jump any higher than his shoulder height. Heavy-bodied breeds (such as Bassets and Newfoundlands) shouldn't jump any higher than two thirds of their shoulder height.

Some athletic breeds can jump one and a half to two times their height with no problems. If your dog is very athletic and very fit, it's fun to try that once in a while, but don't ask him to do it often. The potential for injury is too much.

Be aware of the surface where you're asking your dog to jump. The best is soft, level grass that will provide traction and will also cushion the landings, but other surfaces such as loose dirt or sand are also okay. Just make sure your dog has good traction and will not slip while taking off or landing, and make sure the landing surface is not hard. Asphalt or concrete is too hard; your dog may injure his shoulders after repeated landings.

> **Down, Boy!**
> Dogs with leg, hip, elbow, or back problems should not be asked to Jump until they have been examined by their veterinarian. Low jumping can be good for many dogs, building muscle tone and strength, but get your veterinarian's okay before beginning any of these tricks.

Jumping Over a Stick

This trick teaches your dog the command to *Jump* which, once known, can be easily transferred to other objects. In addition, once your dog knows how to jump the stick, it can be used as a trick by itself or in conjunction with other tricks as part of a trick routine.

> **Dog Talk**
> The command to **Jump** can be "Fido, Jump" or "Fido, hup."

You will need a jumping stick for this trick. A 48-inch-long dowel that is one inch in diameter (found in hardware stores, craft stores, or lumber yards) works well. You can paint the dowel white for visibility or use colored duct tape to make stripes on it. You will also want to have some good treats.

1. Have your dog Sit by your left side in the Heel position. Hold the stick in your left hand and treats in your right.

2. Tell your dog to Stay and take a couple of steps away from him, then turn and face his path of travel should he walk straight ahead.

3. Place the stick ahead of you diagonally across the dog's path of travel—that is, with the tip of it on the ground and your hand holding it. (Imagine using the stick to point out something on the ground.) Hold the stick at about one quarter the dog's height at the shoulders.

4. Show your dog the treat in your right hand on the far side of the stick and encourage him to come get it.

5. When he begins to jump (or step over) the stick, tell him "Fido, Jump!" and praise him. (Do not tell him the command before he does it or he may go around or stop, thereby learning those words mean something else.)

6. Repeat for five repetitions and take a break.

Troubleshooting

If your dog hesitates to go over the stick, drop it to the ground and Heel over it several times. Show him the stick is harmless.

Repeat these steps for several training sessions over several days. When your dog is moving easily toward the stick and is hopping over it, hold the stick completely parallel to the ground at the same height as before.

At this point you can also begin decreasing the hand signal with the treat. Most dogs take enough pleasure in jumping that they usually don't continue to need a food reward. The jumping and verbal praise are enough.

When the dog no longer requires the treat and hand signal, and is jumping easily, begin moving the stick around. Hold it in front of you, to the side, and bring it down in front of the dog as he's heeling. You can also increase the height now. Teach your dog to hop over it wherever he sees it and hears the Jump command. Be liberal with your praise.

> **BARK** **Troubleshooting**
>
> If your dog tries to duck under the stick, you're making it too high too soon. Lower it, get your dog jumping it again, and then increase the height very gradually.

Jumping Through a Hoop

When your dog can jump a stick easily (the easiest of the jumping tricks), you can teach him to jump through a hoop. The command to Jump is the same as for the stick.

I use the plastic hoops found in toy stores for $3 to $5. Some are Hula Hoops™ although some are sold under other names. Some of the hoops have little things inside the plastic hoop that make rattling noises. If the hoops you buy do, you'll have to introduce your dog to the hoop and its noises before you teach him to jump through it. If you don't introduce him to the noise, your dog may be startled by it and will avoid the hoop.

To introduce your dog to the hoop, put it on the ground and walk him over it several times. Then kick the hoop, making it move and rattle, and then walk your dog over it again. Ask your dog to Heel and carry the hoop in your right hand, keeping it still at first and then swinging it so it rattles. When your dog doesn't care about it anymore, you can start your jumping training.

You will need one hoop and some treats.

1. Have your dog Sit in the Heel position. Tell him to Stay and walk a couple steps ahead of him, then turn to face his line of travel.

2. Hold the hoop in your left hand with the bottom resting on the ground.

3. Hold a treat in your right hand and place it at your dog's nose level in the center of the hoop.

4. Encourage your dog to come get it.

5. As he begins to hop or step through the hoop, tell him, "Fido, Jump!" and pull your hand back so he comes all the way through. Praise and reward him.

6. Repeat for a total of five repetitions and give him a break.

Repeat these steps for several training sessions over several days. You will find your dog picking this up very quickly; after all, he did the same thing with the stick, so he's already comfortable with the Jump command. As soon as he's jumping easily, decrease and then stop the treat and hand signal. Emphasize your verbal command and praise.

When he's jumping easily and is not trying to avoid the hoop, begin moving it around, just like you did with the stick. Vary the hoop's position and height and encourage your dog to jump through wherever you hold it.

Troubleshooting

If your dog is hesitant to jump through the hoop, you can use a stick to give him confidence. Use one hand to hold a hoop upright and then the other hand to place the stick across the bottom of it. Encourage your dog to jump the stick.

The stick and hoop can be combined to make multiple jumping opportunities.

Jumping Through Your Arms

Although jumping through a hoop is great fun and quite amusing (we do watch the big cats jump through hoops at the circus!), jumping through your arms is even more spectacular.

The command is the same as it was for the stick and hoop, "Fido, Jump." To begin this trick, your dog must be jumping through the hoop easily no matter where the hoop is held.

You need a hoop for the first few training steps. No treats are needed; your praise will be your dog's reward.

1. Have your dog Sit a few steps away from you.

2. Kneel down or bend over and hold the hoop close to your body so one edge is touching you.

3. Send your dog through the hoop, "Fido, Jump!"

4. Praise him as he's jumping.

5. Repeat for a total of five repetitions.

6. Kneel down or bend over, and hold the hoop so it's touching your body and curve your arms so that one is lying along the bottom of the hoop and the other is along the top of the hoop.

7. Send your dog through the hoop (and your arms) and praise him as he's jumping.

8. Repeat for a total of five repetitions.

Repeat these training steps over several training sessions for several days. When your dog is jumping well with no detours around your arms and the hoop, and with no hesitation, you can move on to the next training steps.

9. Have your dog Sit a few steps away from you.

10. Kneel down or bend over, and curve your arms as if you were holding the hoop, making a big circle, but keep your arms open (don't close the circle). You want to give your dog lots of room.

11. Send your dog through your arms, "Fido, Jump!"

12. Praise him as he jumps.

13. Repeat for a total of five repetitions.

BARK Troubleshooting
If your dog hesitates to jump through your arms, go back to the hoop and repeat all the steps again, taking more time at the steps where your arms are curved with the hoop. Stay at those training steps until your dog's hesitation disappears.

Repeat these training steps over a couple of weeks until your dog is jumping easily through your arms. Then, and only then, close your circle, linking your hands together, if your dog is small enough to fit through the circle.

Jumping Over People

Motorcycles can jump over school buses, so why can't your dog jump over people? He can! This is a great trick as long as you can find some human volunteers.

You need a jumping stick and a human volunteer.

1. Have your human volunteer lie on the ground face down.

2. Have your dog Sit a few steps away from the volunteer, and then hold the jumping stick horizontally immediately in front of the volunteer.

3. Tell your dog, "Fido, Jump!" and praise him as he jumps over the stick and the volunteer.

4. Repeat for a total of five repetitions and take a break.

Repeat for several training sessions over several days.

When your dog is jumping well, with no hesitation, you can move on to your next training steps.

5. Have your volunteer lie on the ground, face down, and have your dog Sit several steps away.

6. With your dog watching you, place the jumping stick on your volunteer's back and leave it there.

7. Send your dog over the human jump, "Fido, Jump!" and praise him as he's jumping. (If he lands on your volunteer, withhold any additional praise.)

8. Repeat for a total of five repetitions and give your dog a break.

9. At your next training session, repeat steps 5 through 7 five times.

10. Now have your volunteer lie down on the ground, face down, but do not use the jumping stick. Send your dog over the human jump and praise him as he's jumping.

11. Repeat for a total of five repetitions and then stop for a while.

Repeat these steps over several days. Later, when you know your dog will jump easily and without hesitation, you can ask your volunteer to position himself on his hands and knees and have your dog jump over him.

BARK Troubleshooting
Some dogs are worried about jumping over people. If your dog is, take a couple of pillows and dress them in your clothes. Have your dog jump this fake person for a while and then try it again with a live volunteer.

When your dog is jumping well over someone lying on the ground, you can ask your helpers to come up to their hands and knees.

Jumping Over Another Dog

This can be a great trick when you have two cooperative dogs. You need one that can hold a very secure Down Stay and another that is confident enough to jump over his buddy. This is best done with dogs who know each other well and get along. Dogs who play together will usually cooperate with this trick.

Down, Boy!

Don't ask a timid, shy, or fearful dog to jump over another dog, especially a bolder one. The bolder dog will probably protest and make the timid dog even more fearful.

The dog doing the Down Stay needs to be very good at this command, even with lots of distractions, so practice this a lot. Remember to use lots of praise and rewards as you step up the difficulty of the Stay.

1. Have him Down Stay while someone walks around him, steps over him, and makes noise.

2. Make sure he can hold the Down Stay while the other dog is heeling and being praised.

3. Have him hold it, too, while the other dog is jumping over a stick and being praised for that.

4. The dog doing the jumping should be jumping the stick very well, and needs to have a good understanding of the Jump command.

When both dogs are ready, you can put the act together.

5. The owner of the dog doing the Down should have her dog lie down and stay, and then step to her dog's head.

6. The owner of the jumping dog should have her dog Sit a few steps away from the down dog.

7. She should then step to the down dog and hold the jumping stick next to the down dog, horizontal to the ground, at about the height of the down dog's back.

8. She should then send her dog, "Fido, Jump!" and praise him as he's jumping.

9. Praise and release the down dog.

10. Repeat for a total of five repetitions.

Troubleshooting

If the dog doing the Down Stay is unsure about holding the Stay, his owner can kneel in front of him, keeping one hand on his collar and encouraging him to do a Watch Me. When he does, praise him for watching and for ignoring the dog doing the jumping.

After several training sessions over several days, when both dogs are cooperating and have relaxed, remove the jumping stick and ask the jumping dog to jump over the down dog without it. If the jumping dog hesitates, bring the stick back but place it on the ground next to the down dog. You can then make it disappear quickly!

The dog (or dogs) doing the Down Stay must be able to hold it with any kind of distractions and the dog doing the jumping must be confident enough to jump the other dog or dogs.

This trick can turn into other tricks. You can have your dog jump two dogs lying next to each other, or a dog and a child. You can also teach several dogs to play leap frog. Have two or three lie down with landing space in between each, and have one jump each one in succession. Then have the jumping dog lie down at the end of the line and have each of the others take their turn jumping and adding to the line. It's fast, requires good training skills, and looks very impressive.

The Least You Need to Know

- 🐾 Tricks that require thought and movement can keep busy dogs out of trouble!

- 🐾 Bow and Say Your Prayers are fun tricks while Spin and Dance are great for active dogs.

- 🐾 Make sure you keep your dog safe from harm as you teach him to Jump.

- 🐾 There are several ways to vary the jumping tricks, with a stick, a hoop, people, and other dogs.

7

Active Tricks for the Agile Dog

In This Chapter

🏠 Teaching your dog to Heel on both sides

🏠 Training your dog to Back and to Follow

🏠 Introducing the Weave

🏠 Weaving through poles, hoops, and legs

The tricks introduced in this chapter are great for dogs who are active and like to move. Although you will want to teach the tricks slowly, after your dog understands, these tricks are best done quickly. When performed with enthusiasm, your audience will be wowed!

Training Heel and Other Side

This trick will have your dog moving from the Heel position on your left side to the same position on your right side, which I call *Other Side*, and then back again. When the dog understands this trick, he can go from one side to the other every few steps as you walk. When performed with precision and enthusiasm, this is a very impressive trick.

Before beginning this trick, go back to Chapter 2 and review your dog's training skills for the Watch Me and Heel. Your dog should do a very good Watch Me on command, and should walk nicely in the Heel position, with his shoulder by your left leg. When your dog is doing the Heel and Watch Me reliably, review the off-leash skills in Chapter 3.

Dog Talk _____
Other Side means the Heel position (the dog's neck and shoulder next to your leg), but on your right side instead of the left.

The only equipment you need for this trick is a leash and some really good treats. This is the time to dig out those special treats—the freeze-dried liver or diced cheese. The good treats will help focus your dog's attention on you and will serve as a good lure.

1. Begin by having your dog Sit by your left side in the Heel position, with the leash on him. You're going to have him move from your left side to your right, passing behind you, as you walk forward.

2. Have both the leash and the treat in your left hand.

3. Show your dog the treat as you tell him, "Fido, Watch Me!" Praise him.

4. Tell your dog, "Fido, Heel" and walk forward, slowly, so you can coordinate your actions.

5. Pass your left hand behind your back, transferring the leash and treat to your right hand as you tell your dog, "Fido, Other Side."

6. As soon as your dog begins to follow your hand, praise him so he knows he's doing the right thing.

7. Bring your right hand (and your dog) forward so the dog is walking in the Heel position on your right side.

8. As soon as your dog reaches that position, praise him enthusiastically and pop the treat in his mouth.

Troubleshooting

If your dog Heels well, he might be reluctant to move from the Heel position. In these instances, walk forward after saying "Watch Me" and do not say "Heel." Use the treat to lure your dog behind you as you say "Fido, Other Side." As soon as your dog begins to move, praise him!

If your dog is reliable off leash and does a very good Watch Me, you can train this trick off leash, moving the treat behind you from hand to hand. It's a little easier than transferring the leash, too. However, if your dog is not attentive to you, or is easily distracted, use the leash.

Down, Boy!

Be careful with toy breeds when training this trick. Most learn to steer clear of walking feet. Make sure your tiny dog doesn't get kicked or stepped on.

9. Practice for several training sessions just having your dog move from the left side to the right side. When your dog understands and is moving without hesitation, begin to decrease the hand signal.

10. Begin with a treat in each hand, and your dog off leash or with his leash folded and tucked into his collar so that you and your dog both can move freely.

11. Tell your dog "Fido, Watch Me." When you have his attention, say "Fido, Heel" and walk forward. Praise him as he does.

12. After a few steps, say "Fido, Other Side" and move your left hand backward as you've been doing.

13. As your dog moves back, reach back with your right hand, showing your dog the lure in that hand, and at the same time bring your left hand forward. By doing this (and not handing the treat from hand to hand), you are decreasing the left hand signal.

14. With the right hand, bring the dog up into position on your
    right side, praise him, and pop the treat in his mouth.

As your dog gains more confidence, you can decrease the hand
signals until you can simply move one finger on your left or right
hand (a flick of the finger) as you give the verbal commands and
your dog will change position.

When your dog will move from the Heel position (on the left)
to the Other Side position (on the right) easily, without the leash,
and showing no signs of confusion, you can teach him to move from
the right side back to the left. This is usually much easier, as he
already understands what "Heel" means and where the Heel position is. Use the same training steps as you did before, simply reversing them.

The dog begins on the left side, in a nice Heel position,
and then ends up on the right side.

When your dog will go back and forth from the left side to the right, and then back again on command, you can speed things up. Ask your dog to transfer sides every ten steps or so. As your dog gets better and gains confidence, he can change sides even more quickly. Kelsey, a yellow Labrador Retriever owned by Rick Hawes of Oceanside, California, can change sides every other step. She does so enthusiastically, head up, tail wagging furiously, watching Rick intently. Rick says, "This is one of Kelsey's favorite tricks, and she can bounce back and forth almost as fast as I can give her the command and signal. I think one of the reasons she likes it so much is because it's fast; we have a lot of fun with it, and this trick never gets boring for her."

Introducing Back

This trick teaches your dog to back away from you, while watching you, and backing straight without turning. Although a very simple trick when performed by itself, *Back* is a trick that is often combined with other tricks when putting together a routine.

You will need some props for this trick. Two picnic table benches would work, or a couple of concrete blocks to elevate two 2 × 4 boards, six to eight feet long. You will also need your dog's leash and some treats for rewards.

 Dog Talk
Back means to back up in a straight line, without turning around.

1. Position the benches or boards parallel to each other lengthwise, just wide enough so you can walk between them. If your dog is small or short, position the benches on their sides. The benches or boards will guide your dog as you teach this trick.

2. With your dog on leash, position yourself and your dog between the benches. Have your dog stand in front of you, facing you, and tell him "Fido, Watch Me!"

3. Tell your dog "Fido, Back!" as you step toward him. When he backs up a step, praise him and pop a treat in his mouth.

4. Repeat the exercise, praising each step.

5. When he takes a step on his own upon hearing your command (without you stepping toward him), give him a jackpot reward!

Very gradually increase the number of steps (up to five or six) you ask him to take before rewarding him.

Troubleshooting — Do not use a hand signal with a treat (lure) over your dog's head to signal him to Back. This will cause your dog's head to come up and hips to go down; he will Sit. Instead, use your verbal command, "Fido, Back." If you wish to use a hand signal, make the signal at or below your dog's eye level.

Troubleshooting — If, without the props, your dog begins to back away and turn, or Backs crookedly, practice next to something that can serve as a guideline, such as the wall of a house, a park bench, or even a high curb.

When your dog is backing up nicely, without hesitation, on command, remove one of the barriers or benches and continue to practice using the remaining barrier as a guide. After several days of practice, if there is no problem, remove the other bench or board.

When your dog will back up five or six steps with no problem, begin combining Back with other commands. Have him Stand, Back, Sit, Down, and Come, praising and rewarding each command. As your dog learns more tricks, you can mix in the Back with those, too. For example, a therapy dog in front of a group of nursing home residents could Stand, Back on command, and then Bow in front of the residents. Imagine the applause!

Training Follow Me

This trick will teach your dog to walk directly behind you, following closely, as if shadowing you. It's a fun trick and looks as if you and your dog are playing follow the leader. Although in the beginning you will be simply walking forward, when your dog understands this trick you can make it more difficult, walking in circles, zigzags, or making about turns. It's great fun and challenging for your dog.

The *Follow Me* can be tough to teach initially because most dogs want to watch our face during training. Be patient, use some really good treats for lures, and give your dog time to learn what you're asking him to do.

The only props you need for this trick are your dog's leash and some treats to use as lures and rewards.

Dog Talk _____

Follow Me means walk directly behind me and follow me wherever I go.

1. Begin with your dog on leash.

2. Hold your dog's leash in one hand and the treats in another. Let your dog smell the treats.

3. Turn your back on your dog, place both hands together behind your back, letting your dog see and smell where the treats are being held, and take a few steps forward as you tell your dog, "Fido, Follow Me."

4. If he hesitates and the leash tightens, encourage him, "Come on! Follow Me!" without turning to face him.

5. If you feel his nose on your hand with the treat, let him take a small piece as long as you're both moving forward, and praise him, "Good boy!"

BARK **Troubleshooting** _____

Most dogs prefer to watch your face during training, and that makes this trick hard. Be careful not to turn and look at your dog while training this trick or he'll continue to try to see your face. Keep your face turned away and praise and reward him without looking at him.

As he learns what you want, and follows you willingly, walk a few steps more before rewarding him.

BARK) Troubleshooting

If your dog continues to try to walk by your side instead of behind you, use the benches or barriers you used for the Back trick. Use the preceding training steps while walking between the barriers with your dog following you.

After your dog understands the trick and gets better at following you, gradually make it more challenging. As you walk, incorporate turns, circles, zigzags, and about turns into your trick routine. Just increase the difficulty slowly, making sure you don't lose your dog as you move, and encouraging him to follow you.

Teaching the Weave

The *Weave* command teaches your dog to wind through a variety of objects, curving his body, and to alternate directions as he does. The easiest way to teach the Weave is to use upright poles, but when your dog can do this trick, you can teach him to weave through poles, hula hoops, and even your legs.

The trick-training Weave is similar to the Weave for agility competition. In agility, however, the dog must enter the weave poles in a specific position, and must move through the poles rapidly. In trick training, neither entry position nor speed are important. In addition, in trick training, we will use the Weave for more than just poles. So if you're also training your dog in agility, don't worry about the differences; this Weave is just for fun!

Your dog will need to know the Watch Me command for this trick and will need to be able to come to you reliably when you call him.

Dog Talk

The **Weave** is always done with some obstacles, either poles, hoops, legs, or other objects that your dog can move around in a figure eight or serpentine pattern.

You will need some props for the Weave, including a dozen 24-inch-long plant stakes, either wooden or plastic, and a dozen 36-inch-long pieces of plastic pipe (all available at any hardware store). The pipe should be a wide enough diameter to slip over the plant stakes.

The plant stakes will be pounded into the ground, and the pipes set over the stakes. The pipes, being white plastic, are easier to see than the stakes, and because they are simply set over the stakes and are not fastened down, can slip and turn as your dog brushes up against them, creating less stress and resistance.

Down, Boy!

Although any dog of any breed or size can learn to Weave, it does require body agility and movement in the neck and shoulders, and could stress rapidly growing puppies or dogs with preexisting conditions such as arthritis.

Moving Through the Poles

To introduce your dog to the idea of moving through the weave poles, pound six of them into the ground, about eighteen inches apart, in a straight line. Make a second line of weave poles about eighteen inches from the first line, so that you have two parallel lines of poles, making a narrow lane.

1. Have a friend or family member hold your dog at one end of the two lines of poles. (Don't leave him in a Sit Stay, as you want him to be excited to come to you between the poles.) As you leave your dog, show him (and let him sniff) a really good treat.

2. Get him excited as you leave him, "Do you want this? I've got a treat!"

3. Go to the other end of the lines of poles and place yourself between the last two poles, directly opposite your dog.

4. Using an excited, happy tone of voice, call your dog to come, "Fido, Come! Yeah! Good boy!" (Make sure your friend knows to release your dog as you call him.)

5. As your dog dashes between the two lines of poles, praise him! When he reaches you, continue praising and pop that treat in his mouth.

Troubleshooting

If your dog appears to be concerned about moving through the poles, even when you call him, run him through a few times on leash, with both of you moving between the lines of poles.

6. Do this five times. When your dog is showing no problem running through the weave poles, reposition the poles so they are shoulder width apart and do this again five times.

Zigzagging Through the Poles

Have at hand some good treats to use as a lure, and begin with your dog on a leash. Pound four stakes into the ground in a straight line, about eighteen inches from each other. Slip a plastic pipe over each.

1. Have your dog in the Heel position with the both of you standing in front of the first pole. Have the dog's leash in your left hand and treats in your right hand.

2. Step toward the gap between the first and second pole, and reaching around the second pole, show your dog the treat so he steps between the poles. At the same time tell him, "Fido, Weave."

3. Using the treat, draw him around the second pole, praising him as you do. The treat is the lure to bring your dog around the pole and the hand movement is going to become a hand signal, which will mean Weave.

4. As he steps around the pole, make sure his leash doesn't get caught.

5. Continue in this manner, keeping your hand one pole ahead of him so you can lead him around each pole.

6. Praise him as he steps toward and around each pole.

7. When he finishes the fourth pole, praise him enthusiastically and pop the treat in his mouth.

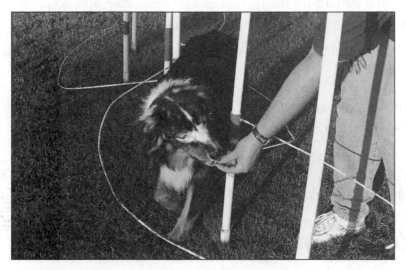

Let your dog follow the lure through the poles as you encourage him. Stiff wire can help create a path between poles for your dog to follow.

8. Repeat this exercise three or four times and stop, giving your dog a break. Pet him, praise him, and throw the ball for him. Then go back to the poles and try it again. After several days of this routine, he should be weaving through the poles, following your hand, with more confidence.

9. Add two more weave poles to the line.

10. Take your dog's leash off, or fold it and tuck it under his collar.

11. Continue using the treat in hand as a lure, but move a little more quickly, using your voice to encourage your dog to follow, "Weave! Good boy! Yeah!"

12. When he finishes the line of poles, praise him and pop that treat in his mouth.

Over the next few weeks, gradually add more poles until your dog is weaving through all twelve. As you add poles, continue using the hand signal with the treat in front of your dog, and keep the excitement level high with praise and encouragement.

When your dog can Weave through all twelve poles easily, with no hesitation, keep the treat in your pocket while giving the hand signal for the Weave. The hand signal can be as simple as pointing to the spot between the poles where you want your dog to Weave. Give him the treat after he finishes all twelve poles.

Eventually, as your dog gains confidence, you will be able to point at the line of weave poles and simply say, "Fido, Weave," and your dog will zigzag through the entire line of poles.

Weaving Through Hoops

Plastic hoops, like hula hoops, are great toys to use with canine trick training. Not only can your dog learn to jump through them (as was taught in Chapter 6), but if you anchor six hoops upright, end to end, your dog can also Weave through them. This is much more colorful than simple weave poles, and you can make it more exciting by elevating the hoops so your dog must jump through each hoop as he Weaves.

For this trick, you need six plastic hoops, seven plant stakes tall enough to anchor the hoops, and some duct tape. Begin with three hoops and four stakes. Pound one stake into the ground; stand a hoop upright next to it and tape them together so that they look like the number 10. The bottom of the hoop should rest on the ground. Pound the second stake into the ground on the opposite side of that hoop, and tape that

BARK Troubleshooting — Jumping and weaving through the hoops is more difficult than simply weaving through the poles, so always teach your dog to Weave through the poles first. After he has mastered the weave poles, introduce him to the hoops.

side (like the number 101). That first hoop should now be stable. Stand the second hoop upright and tape it to the second stake. Continue in this manner until three hoops are set up, end to end in a straight line, with a stake at each side and at each end of the line of hoops (so that you have 1010101).

Your dog already knows the Weave command, but knows it with poles. He will not immediately understand that the command can apply to other things, especially something that looks as weird as this line of hoops, so skip any preparatory steps and get right to training the trick.

1. To introduce your dog to the idea that he can go through the hoops, toss a treat through the center of a hoop. When he goes through the hoop after the treat, praise him.

2. Offer him a treat and call him back through, "Fido, Come!" and praise him when he comes back to you. When he will bounce through with no hesitation, you can begin weaving.

3. Position your dog and yourself facing the first hoop so that you can reach over or through to signal your dog to go through the hoop, "Fido, Weave!"

4. Be ready to move him toward the second hoop, repeating the command. The hoops are bigger around than the poles were set apart, so your timing and position to work your dog will be different.

5. Guide him through the second and third hoops in the same manner, using the treat and hand signal.

6. Praise him enthusiastically as he moves through the hoops, and pop that treat in his mouth when he finishes the third hoop.

Use treats as a lure to guide your dog through each hoop.

Your dog will pick up the weave hoops much more quickly than he did the weave poles because he already understands what Weave means. As he gains confidence, you can add more hoops, one at a time, and when he's weaving through all six hoops well, you can also slowly decrease your hand signal, just as you did for the weave poles.

After your dog has had some time to get used to all six hoops, and when you can use a hand signal to guide him without having to lead him through the hoops, you can make this more interesting. Refasten the hoops on the stakes so they are a couple of inches off the ground. Now your dog will have to hop slightly as he weaves. This adds a whole new element to the trick!

Down, Boy!

Jumping and weaving through the hoops requires strength, balance, and agility. Keep the jump height low, no more than half his leg height.

Before asking him to Weave, have him jump through a few times so he's aware of the new height. Then ask him to Weave. Don't laugh at him if he trips or stumbles a few times; he's concentrating on his Weave. The elevated hoops require him to concentrate on both his steps and his Weave.

If you have an athletic dog who enjoys jumping, you can gradually increase the height of the hoops so he jumps a little each time. This can be an eye-catching athletic trick.

Weaving Through Your Legs

Weaving through your legs is a great trick that isn't as difficult as it looks. Because fewer props are needed than the other weaving tricks (no poles and no hoops), it's a good trick for therapy dogs and a good trick to "take on the road."

As with weaving through the hoops, teaching your dog to Weave through the poles first is recommended. It's much easier to teach the concept of weaving with poles that are easy to set up and comfortable for you to reach around, than it is to bend, twist, and distort your body.

> **BARK** **Troubleshooting**
> If you have trouble with your back or legs, or if you have poor balance, skip this trick. This trick requires the dog owner to step high and carefully, and to bend and twist.

The only things you need for this trick are some good treats to serve as lures and rewards.

1. Begin with your dog sitting in the Heel position, off leash. Have some treats in each hand.

2. Take an exaggerated step forward with your right foot so that there is a big gap between your legs. Tell your dog, "Fido, Weave Legs!" as you bring the treat down behind that leg. Move your hand so your dog sees it. Praise him as he moves toward and behind your leg.

3. Lead your dog behind the right leg and forward.

4. As your dog follows your hand forward around your right leg, take an exaggerated step forward with your left foot.

5. Using a treat in your left hand, bring your dog behind your left leg so that you are sketching a figure eight shape.

Down, Boy!

If you have a large- or giant-breed dog, encourage him to duck or crouch as he goes under and between your legs. Don't allow your dog to move you, lift you, or bowl you over.

6. When your dog comes up on your left side, praise him enthusiastically and pop the treat in his mouth.

7. Continue until your dog is comfortable making the figure eight.

As your dog is watching your hand, move it behind you so the dog drops back. The next step will be to bring him behind and then between your legs.

When your dog is weaving comfortably, you can make some changes in the trick. For a Standing Weave, stand with your legs apart but even under your shoulders and have your dog do a figure eight around your legs. For a Walking Weave, step forward and have your dog Weave through each step.

The Weave through the legs is an eye-catching trick that will leave your audience amazed.

The Least You Need to Know

- 🏠 The tricks in this chapter require your dog to pay attention, move quickly, and be agile and athletic.

- 🏠 Use lures to show your dog where you want him to move, praise him enthusiastically, and always reward him with that treat.

- 🏠 The Heel, Other Side, and Follow Me tricks all originate with good walking-on-the-leash skills.

- 🏠 When your dog knows how to Weave through the poles, he can also Weave through hoops and your legs.

Chapter 8

Let's Have Some Fun!

In This Chapter

- Introducing the sneeze and kiss
- Ringing the bells
- Some tricks are also games
- The touch is a trick and training

This chapter introduces some different types of tricks, such as the sneeze and kiss, that are fun to train and use. These will also amaze your friends because you can direct your dog to do them, "Fido, give Grandma a kiss!" or "Fido, did you sneeze?" People will think your dog understands every word you say.

Some tricks have more practical uses, as ringing the bells does, and other tricks are also games. Have you seen some of the old movies with the con man playing the shell game? He hides a coin under an inverted bowl next to two other inverted bowls and then shuffles them around. If the child or country bumpkin can locate the coin, he can keep it. This chapter will show you how to teach your dog the shell game. There's lots of laughter in this chapter.

Sneezes on Cue

Your dog sneezes to clear his nose, just as you do, but he also sneezes as a means of communication. Dogs sneeze when they're excited, particularly when something is funny. You can take advantage of this when you're training by acting silly and making a big fuss over your dog. Tickle his tummy, roll over, roll yourself over, laugh, and wait for that sneeze to happen. When it does, praise him, "Sneeze! Good boy!" Eventually he will recognize the command Sneeze and respond with one of his own. But some dogs will mimic your sneeze and you can use this to help you train this as a trick.

Bet You Didn't Know

Dogs sneeze more when they're excited than when they're calm, so make a big fuss over your dog when you're training the Sneeze.

Down, Boy!

If your dog won't mimic your sneeze, try blowing on his nose—but be careful. Some dogs like to snap at blowing air; make sure your face isn't in the way!

1. Sit on the floor in front of your dog. Have some good treats in hand.

2. Sneeze (fake sneeze, of course!) in your dog's face.

3. If he sneezes back, praise him, "Sneeze! Good! Yeah!" and pop a treat in his mouth.

4. If he doesn't sneeze, wait a few seconds (giving him time to think) and then sneeze again.

5. If you can repeat this four more times, do so.

When you are with your dog, praise him when he Sneezes, even if it's only to clear his nose. "Sneeze! Good!" Eventually, he will come to understand that the word *Sneeze* applies to that action.

Giving Kisses

My five-year-old Australian Shepherd, Riker, loves to give kisses. I can turn him toward someone, anyone, and tell him, "Give Kisses" and that poor soul is covered in doggy kisses! Any exposed skin will be licked. Now obviously, not everyone enjoys doggy kisses, especially such enthusiastic ones, so I'm careful about this. But if the person is a friend who likes Riker, this is a trick Riker truly loves to do.

This is a very easy trick to teach. You need some soft food, like a piece of hot dog or cheese, and a willing volunteer. Kids often like to participate in this dog training.

1. Take that bit of soft food and rub it on the skin of your volunteer (on the arm is good).

2. Tell your dog, "Give Kisses!" in a happy tone of voice and let him sniff the skin.

3. When he licks, praise him, "Good boy to give kisses!"

4. Make him stop licking, call him away, and praise him again.

5. Repeat for a total of five repetitions.

After your dog understands the kiss command, and, when he hears it, is going directly to the person to sniff and lick, begin decreasing the amount of food you rub on your volunteer. Within several training sessions, just touch the food to the volunteer's skin. Your dog should continue to lick.

 **Down, Boy!**

Some dogs get a little too excited when doing this trick and will put some teeth behind it. Watch for this (ask your volunteer to tell you), and if he gets too excited, take him away and let him calm down.

At this point, you can decide where you want your dog to Give Kisses. Most people would prefer to not be licked in the face, but behind the ear is usually okay. Or you can keep your dog focused on the arm. It's up to you. If you want to change the focus to behind the ear, simply rub the food behind the ear and help your dog find it there. As soon as he begins sniffing and licking, tell him, "Give Kisses!" and praise him, "Good boy!"

Giving Kisses is a sweet (although sometimes slobbery) trick.

Learning Left from Right

Dogs can learn their left from their right, and can use that in many dog sports, including carting and agility. In trick training, you can use this in conjunction with other tricks, or to impress your audience with how smart your dog is. After all, some *people* have a hard time remembering which hand is right or left, so when your dog knows, well, that's smart!

To teach this trick, you need some smelly treats (like hot dogs) or a very special toy or ball.

1. Begin with your dog sitting by your side in the Heel position. When he's on your left side, it's easier to teach him to go right, so start with that direction first.

2. Let your dog sniff the smelly treat or see the toy or ball in your right hand, and then move your hand away from him, encouraging him to follow the lure.

3. As he steps forward, move your hand across in front of you, turning your dog toward your right, and say "Fido, Go Right!"

4. Toss the treat or ball as you praise him.

5. Call him back and repeat the process for a total of five repetitions.

Troubleshooting

If your dog does not move from the Sit or hesitates to follow your hand signal, put a leash on him and hold it in the hand with the treat or ball. This can help him follow your hand. When you send him after the ball or treat, either move with him to keep him going or drop the leash.

Some people have trouble remembering their right from left; they will think your dog is a genius!

Continue this way for several training sessions over several days or even a couple of weeks. In addition, every time you take your dog for a walk and make a right turn, tell him, "Fido, Go Right," and when he does, praise him. When you see him beginning to move toward the right on his own upon hearing your command, give him a jackpot of praise and treats!

When your dog is easily moving to the right when he hears the command, you can begin teaching him what Left means. Follow the same training steps for Left as you did for Right, except hold the treat or ball in your left hand. As you signal left, you will move your hand in front of your dog, turning him toward the left. If your dog has some hesitation and you need to step with him, take a step in to your left in front of your dog.

Down, Boy!

Don't add Left to your training until your dog fully understands the Right command. It will only confuse him.

As you teach the Left command, stop working on Right for a while. Don't worry, he won't forget what it means; you just want him to concentrate on Left as he's learning it.

When your dog knows both directions, begin using them. If you're walking down the street, let your dog walk ahead of you a bit (without pulling) and aim for an obstacle (a trash can, light pole, or mailbox) and when you approach it, tell your dog which direction to go around it. If he moves in the correct direction, praise him enthusiastically! If he doesn't, stop, restrain him from going the wrong way, and repeat the command. When he moves correctly, allow him to continue and praise him!

I do this all the time with my dogs. I will walk two or three dogs and allow them to walk ahead of me. When we come to a tree or mailbox, I tell them Right or Left and we all move in unison. I have heard other walkers mutter to themselves, "Wow! Did you see that?" It's great fun!

Bobbing for Dog Biscuits

Bobbing for dog biscuits (or tennis balls) is a great activity for multiple dogs. If your therapy dog group is having a picnic or party, or the local humane society is having a fund-raiser, this is good fun.

You will need a few props for this trick. First, you need a shallow container that holds water. A brand-new plastic kitty litter pan works well. (Later, when your dog knows the trick, you will want something a little deeper.) And you need a half dozen tennis balls.

1. Put enough water in the shallow container so the tennis balls move, but not enough so they are floating. Put one ball in the water.

2. Walk your dog up to the container. Pick up the tennis ball, show it to him, and tease him with it, "Do you want this? Do you?" Drop it back in the water.

3. Tell him, "Fido, Get the Ball!"

4. When he does, praise him and throw the ball for him.

5. Repeat for a total of five repetitions. Don't do more, even if your dog loves tennis balls. You want to stop the training session while he's still excited.

6. Repeat the training steps later.

If he's picking up the ball with no hesitation and doesn't seem bothered by the water, put more water in the container so the ball is floating. Drop the ball in and repeat as you did for the first training steps. When your dog will reach in, grab the floating ball, and take it out of the water with no hesitation, drop in several more balls. Encourage him to keep grabbing them, "Yeah! Get the Ball! Get another one! Super dog!"

 **Bet You Didn't Know**

To make a competitive game out of this, have several tennis balls and a stopwatch. Give each dog thirty seconds. The dog who picks up the most balls in that time wins!

If you don't mind a mess, you can also play this game with dog biscuits. Drop a dog biscuit in the water and encourage your dog to grab it. Most dog biscuits float, but many get soft and mushy after too much exposure to water, so this can get ugly. But as messy as it can be, the dogs are often more motivated to grab the dog biscuits than tennis balls. They are also more reluctant to drop them and go for another one, so the Give command is important here. At one of our dog parties, one Golden Retriever grabbed fifteen dog biscuits in thirty seconds, dropping each one on his owner's command before he went for another one. Good dog!

> **BARK Troubleshooting**
> If your dog doesn't want to drop the ball or biscuit on your command, go back to Chapter 3 and review the section on retrieving.

Ringing the Bells

This trick teaches your dog to ring some bells hanging from a doorknob. He can learn to ring them on command or to ring them when he needs to go outside. This is particularly nice for owners who don't want their dogs to bark to go outside.

You need some bells from the craft store. Those with a two-inch diameter work well because they make more noise than smaller bells. Hang the bells from a doorknob so they are at your dog's nose level. Jingle them and let your dog investigate them.

> **Bet You Didn't Know**
> If you want your dog to ring the bells to go outside (to solve some housetraining issues), ask him, "Do you have to go outside?" and encourage him to ring the bells. When he does, open the door and give him the hot dog treat outside.

You also need some good, soft treats; hot dogs work well.

1. Rub one of the bells with a piece of hot dog.

2. Walk your dog to the bell and tell him, "Ring the bell!"

3. When he noses the bell, licking it to get the hot dog off, pop a treat in his mouth and praise him.

4. Walk him away and do it again. Repeat for a total of five repetitions.

When your dog nudges the bells, causing them to ring,
praise him and pop a treat in his mouth.

After a couple of weeks of training, stop rubbing the bells with hot dogs, and instead just touch one bell with a hot dog once a day. After a few days, stop doing even that. But continue praising and rewarding your dog every time he rings the bells on command.

Very gradually, over a few weeks, send your dog to the bells from farther away. Begin just a step or two away, and as he gains confidence, send him from five feet away, then ten feet, then across the room. In three to four weeks, send him to the bells from another room. Just be prepared to walk with him should he hesitate, and always follow him so you can praise and reward him as he rings the bells.

The Shell Game

In this trick, you'll hide something under an upside-down bowl or plant pot. You can hide a ball or a dog biscuit, anything the dog likes, and then you'll move the bowls around. After shuffling the bowls, you'll ask your dog to indicate where the ball or treat is. This version of the shell game is very impressive, especially if those watching actually think your dog is watching the moving bowls. In reality, however, your dog will be using his scenting abilities to find the correct one.

You need three unbreakable bowls or plant pots—unbreakable, because most dogs get excited and knock these around a little. Four-inch-diameter plastic plant pots work very well.

You also want to have some good, smelly treats. Hot dogs, freeze-dried liver, or cheese works well.

1. Sit on the floor with your dog with one pot and a handful of treats.

2. Place a treat under the inverted pot and tell your dog, "Fido, Find It!" Tip the pot slightly so he noses the crack between the pot and the floor.

3. Praise him and let him grab the treat.

4. Repeat for a total of five repetitions and put everything away.

Bet You Didn't Know

At this point your dog is just getting excited; don't be tempted to keep on training. Always stop at five repetitions. By stopping now, you will build more excitement later. Remember: Always leave your dog wanting more.

After several training sessions over a few days, begin setting the pot flat on the floor and encourage your dog to nose it. Don't let him have the treat until he indicates to you the treat is there. He can nose it, paw it, or even knock the pot over. He just needs to give you a very strong signal. When he's doing this, you can move on to the next training steps.

5. Invert a second pot with nothing under it close to the pot you've been working with.

6. Place a treat under the working pot.

7. Do not move the pots at this point.

8. Ask your dog to find the treat, "Fido, Find It!"

9. When he indicates the correct pot, praise him and tip it so he can get the treat.

10. Repeat for a total of five times and take a break.

Do this for several training sessions over several days. At one training session, have the working pot on your right; at the next training session, place it on the left. Then have it in front of the dog or in front of you. You are teaching your dog to use his nose, so make the placement different at each training session.

BARK **Troubleshooting**

If your dog appears stuck or confused, give him some verbal encouragement. If he's discouraged, tip the pot slightly to give him a whiff of the treat. Do not give him the treat until he indicates the correct pot, though.

The shell game is great fun and a play on an old movie scam.

When your dog is finding the treat every time, move on to the next training steps.

11. Have two pots in front of you, side by side.

12. Place a treat under one. (You can let your dog watch you place it.)

13. Without picking up the pots, shuffle them around a couple of times.

14. Ask your dog to find the treat, "Fido, Find It!" Encourage him to sniff each pot.

15. When he indicates the correct pot, let him have the treat as you praise him, "Yeah! Super dog!"

16. Repeat for five repetitions and take a break.

Bet You Didn't Know
After your dog knows this trick, you can substitute a tennis ball or other favorite toy instead of the treat. Train it as you did with the treats.

After several training sessions over a couple of weeks, you can add a third pot. Keep the training upbeat, with lots of praise, and make sure you use some really good treats.

Teaching the Touch

Touch is both a great trick and very useful to other dog activities. Not only is it an active, interesting trick, but many agility trainers use it as a tool for teaching the dog to traverse obstacles correctly.

Dog Talk
Touch means touch your nose to my hand or another indicated target.

The only equipment you need for this trick, in the beginning, is some good treats. Later you will need something else to serve as a target.

1. Have your dog Sit in front of you. Hold the treats in your right hand, leaving your left hand free and empty.

2. Gently touch the tips of the fingers on your left hand to your dog's nose as you tell him, "Fido, Touch!" and then immediately pop a treat in his mouth. Praise him!

3. Repeat for a total of five repetitions, let him take a break and then do five more.

4. Repeat this several times over several days.

5. When your dog is beginning to lean toward your hand in anticipation of the touch (in anticipation of the treat!), stop moving your hand forward and let him move to your hand. Give him the command as he touches your hand, praise him, and pop a treat in his mouth.

6. Repeat for a total of five repetitions, take a break, and then do five more.

> **BARK** **Troubleshooting**
> If your dog begins shying away from your hand, look at your technique. Touch his nose very gently with just the tips of your fingers. Do not swat his nose with your hand.

Gently touch your dog's nose with the tips of your fingers as you tell him, "Fido, Touch! Good boy!"

After a couple of weeks' worth of repetitions, your dog should be moving well to your hand with your hand held close to him. Now begin moving your hand. Move it a few inches to the left or a few inches to the right. Move it up or down. Encourage your dog to move to your hand, no matter where you hold it, and then to come back to you for the treat.

As your dog gets better at the touch, ask him to move to your hand no matter where you hold it.

Troubleshooting

If your dog hesitates to move toward your hand, release him from the Sit and let him stand freely as you do this. Give him verbal encouragement, too, and let him follow your hand as you move it.

When your dog knows this command well, and is touching your hand eagerly, you can begin asking him to Touch other things. Simply follow the preceding training steps, substituting the other item in place of your hand.

For example, if you want your dog to Touch your car keys, but not retrieve them (because if he retrieved them he might carry them off and bury them in the backyard), you can teach him to Touch the car keys.

1. Hold the keys in your hand and tell your dog, "Fido, Touch keys."

2. Now initially your dog is going to Touch your hand. But if you place the keys in your hand so that is difficult, and he must Touch the keys, he will do so. Praise him and pop a treat in his mouth.

3. Follow the training steps outlined above.

When your dog is Touching the keys easily and you can move your hand with the keys in it and your dog will Touch it readily, begin placing the keys on another surface, such as the arm of the sofa, and ask your dog to touch them there. You might need to keep your hand close at first, but as soon as your dog is Touching the keys there, begin moving your hand away. With practice, you should be able to stand away from the keys with your dog moving toward them to Touch them and then back to you for the treat.

In Chapter 9 you and your dog will learn the Name Game (identifying objects by name) and the Find It Game (locating different items). These can both be combined with the Touch, making them each more spectacular.

The Least You Need to Know

🏠 Sneeze and Kiss are fun tricks, good for therapy dogs or just to play with at home.

🏠 Go Right and Go Left are useful tricks that also demonstrate your dog's intelligence!

🏠 Bobbing for biscuits (or tennis balls) is a great game for dog parties.

🏠 Although many of these tricks also serve useful purposes, don't forget to keep them fun.

Part

Tricks for Canine Geniuses

The tricks in this part are not nearly as easy as the ones in Parts 1 and 2. These tricks require you to think, to follow the training steps carefully, and to have patience. But when your dog learns these tricks, all your effort will be worth it.

Just remember to keep the training positive, even when it seems more like work than play. The process (not just the end result) should be enjoyable for both of you. Take joy in watching your dog learn each training step, and pat yourself on the back for your new training skills.

Chapter 9

Giving Everything a Name

In This Chapter

- 🏠 Naming toys is great fun
- 🏠 Naming your things is very useful
- 🏠 Teaching your dog to search
- 🏠 Playing the Name Game and Find It Game

Your dog has already figured out that certain sounds you make have meanings. For example, he knows that "Do you want to go for a walk?" means he will have the leash hooked up to his collar and you and he will walk around the neighborhood. He has no idea that the sounds he is hearing are English, Spanish, or French; he just knows that the sounds that fit a certain pattern have individual meanings.

But your dog has an unlimited capability of learning new meanings for sounds. After all, dogs are verbal creatures, too. When you teach your dog the meanings of words, you can talk to him and communicate more effectively. This can also translate into great trick training!

Everything Has a Name

Your dog might already understand several words. The most common are walk, leash, hungry, treat, cookie, ride in the car, ball, and bone. He should also know commands to relieve himself outside, as well as the basic obedience commands. If you have begun his trick training, he also knows the commands associated with those tricks. Your dog is accumulating a vocabulary.

Bet You Didn't Know
When you talk to your dog, speak in a friendly, casual tone. (Save baby talk for praising him.) Look at him and make eye contact so he pays attention to you. Emphasize certain words as you go about your routine: gate, door, turtle, bird, and so on. He's capable of learning many words through his daily experiences.

Now you want to teach your dog that a variety of different items have names associated with them. Then when you ask your dog to retrieve a specific toy, he can. Or you can ask him to find your car keys, and he will know what *keys* means.

Naming the First Toy

Begin by giving his toys names, because he will be more excited about working with them than he will be with your belongings. Before you begin this training, go back to Chapter 8 and review the Touch trick. Your dog needs to understand Touch very well before you begin naming anything; it's a vital part of the naming tricks and the Name Game.

When you begin this training, you will need four or five different dog toys (and these can include a ball or two), but the toys should be different from each other and have different names. For example, you can have a tennis ball, a Frisbee™, a rope tug toy, a porcupine squeaky toy, and a Planet Dog Orbee™ ball. The toys should be things your dog is excited about and likes to play with.

Any dog, of any size, breed, or body type, can do this training. The smarter dogs tend to do better at it because it does require some thinking, and dogs that retain learned information also have an easier time.

1. Begin this training with one toy. We'll use the rope toy as an example. In a relaxed situation, such as in the backyard or in the living room, have that toy in hand and some really good treats in your pocket.

2. Practice the Touch trick, having your dog Touch your empty hand. When he Touches your hand, praise him and pop a treat in his mouth. Get him enthusiastic about working.

3. Repeat for a total of five repetitions and give him a short break.

4. Take the rope toy in hand and tell your dog, "Fido, Touch rope!"

5. If he Touches your hand but not the rope, withhold your praise and treats and repeat the command. You can try to maneuver your hand so he Touches the rope or you can Touch the rope to his nose.

6. When he Touches the rope, praise him enthusiastically and pop a treat in his mouth.

7. Repeat for a total of five repetitions and give him a short break.

Repeat the first six training steps several times over the next few days, always beginning with step 1 as a warm-up exercise, even if your dog knows the Touch command well. By repeating it, you will cue him as to what will follow.

When your dog is Touching your hand during warm-ups (step 2) and then is Touching the rope on his own in step 6, you're ready to move on.

8. Repeat steps 1 through 6 as warm-ups.

9. With the rope in your hand, move it away from your body (half an arm's length away) and ask your dog to touch it, "Fido, Touch rope!"

10. When he moves to Touch it, praise him, and when he does Touch it, praise him again and pop a treat in his mouth.

11. Repeat for a total of five repetitions and give him a short break.

12. Repeat steps 8 and 9 as warm-ups.

13. Then repeat 8 and 9, but hold the rope an arm's length away.

14. Repeat for a total of five repetitions and take a break.

15. Warm up with a few close Touches of the rope (in front of you, half an arm's length and then an arm's length away).

16. Place the rope on the floor but keep a hand on it. Tell your dog "Fido, Touch rope!"

17. When he moves toward it, praise him, and when he touches it, praise and treat him.

18. Repeat for a total of five repetitions and take a break.

Repeat steps 15 through 17 several times. When your dog is moving to the rope toy on the floor easily, without hesitation, go on to the next step.

Troubleshooting

If your dog hesitates to move, just hold still and be quiet. Let him think a moment. He might be waiting for you to do something. When he gets no response from you, including no praise and no treats, he will try things on his own.

19. Place the rope on the floor an arm's length away and move your hand away, standing or sitting in a natural position. Tell your dog to Touch it.

20. When he moves toward it, praise him, and when he Touches it, give him a jackpot of praise and treats! "Yeah, good job!"

Now play with this trick. Hold the rope close or far away. Place it on the ground, set it on the chair, or drape it over the footstool. Teach your dog to move to the rope and Touch it, then come back to you for the treat. Praise him as he Touches it.

Naming Subsequent Toys

Naming the first toy is easy. It takes quite a few training steps, but you'll see why shortly. But teaching your dog the names of his other toys is sometimes harder. Right now your dog knows that *Touch rope* means to move toward the toy, Touch it, hear the praise, and come back to you for the treat. However, he might not yet know that the sound that makes up the command Rope actually means that particular toy. He might think the sound of the word *rope* means all toys, or all toys held in your hand, or all long ropelike toys. However, you'll discover your dog's level of understanding as you begin teaching him the names of subsequent toys.

For the second toy, choose one that has a very different-sounding name from the first toy. The tennis ball, the Orbee™, or a Frisbee™ is good if you used a rope toy for the first toy.

1. After you have chosen the second toy, put the rope toy away, and have the new toy in hand and some treats in your pocket.

2. Practice a few regular Touches, without using the toy, just having your dog Touch your hand. Praise him well and pop treats in his mouth each time he Touches your hand. Get him excited and enthusiastic about working.

3. Pick up the toy (let's use the ball as an example) and tell your dog, "Fido, Touch ball!"

4. If he Touches the ball, praise him enthusiastically and pop a few treats in his mouth. If he Touches your hand, withhold praise and treats and wait a moment. If he doesn't respond, Touch the ball to his nose.

5. Repeat for a total of five repetitions and take a break.

Repeat these training steps several times over a couple of days. When he is Touching the ball on his own, you're ready to move on.

6. Repeat steps 1 through 4 as warm-ups.

Down, Boy!

You will find that your dog will catch on more quickly with the second toy than the first. Because of this, there are fewer training steps for the second toy. Don't skip ahead, though. Follow these training steps so your dog learns what he needs to know.

7. With the ball in your hand, ask your dog to Touch it at half an arm's length away. Repeat for a total of five repetitions and take a break.

8. When he will touch it at half an arm's length away, hold it an arm's length away and repeat for a total of five repetitions and then take a break.

Over the next several training sessions, continue moving the ball as you did when you trained the first toy—moving it to the floor with your hand on it, and then moving your hand away. Train in gradual increments, moving on to the next step only when your dog is doing the present step well.

When your dog will Touch the ball on the floor when your hand is not touching it, you're ready to move on to the next training step.

9. Now you need both the ball and the rope. Have some treats in your pocket. Sit on the sofa or a chair and have your dog sitting in front of you, facing you.

10. Place the ball behind you and hold the rope in front of you. Do five touches with the rope, praising and rewarding your dog each time.

11. Place the rope behind you and bring out the ball. Do five touches with the ball, praising and rewarding your dog each time.

12. Bring the rope back out and hold it in one hand and the ball in the other hand.

13. Tell your dog to touch the ball "Fido, Touch ball!"

14. If he does, praise him enthusiastically and give him a jackpot of treats! "Good job!" If he hesitates, give him a chance to think. When he moves toward the ball, praise him. If he moves to the rope, be quiet.

Dance, Sophie, Dance!

The Crawl, with an appropriate costume, can be part of a trick routine.

After the dog can Weave through upright poles, he can quickly learn to Weave through hoops and then your legs.

The Shake is an easy trick that can be the foundation for other tricks, including Other Paw and Wave.

Dancing with your dog is great fun!

Costumes can be for more than just Halloween; they are great props for trick routines and good icebreakers for therapy dogs.

Trick training is not just for young dogs; even seniors can learn new tricks. Shasta, at 13, still did the best sneezes!

Cayla doesn't need to wash her face after Sasha's kisses!

Sam says his prayers.

Bailey Touches the triangle shape on command. He knows triangle, heart, circle, and star.

Puppies can learn to wear costumes; just introduce them slowly with lots of positive reinforcements.

Some people are worried about big dogs or dogs of certain breeds. Costumes and tricks can make people laugh and alleviate that worry.

Most dogs will follow a treat wherever it leads.

Trick Training will strengthen the bond between you and your dog.

Most tricks need no special equipment.

Some dogs love to jump and are natural clowns.

Troubleshooting

BARK

This stage of training tells you whether your dog understands that items have individual names or whether he's simply touching whatever you send him to. If he's confused, go back and repeat the training steps, beginning at the start of this chapter, and emphasize the names as you do, "Fido, Touch ROPE! Good boy!"

As you continue training this trick, change where you hold the toys. One time have the rope in your right hand and the ball in your left, and then switch them. Hold the toys directly in front of you or each at arm's length to each side of you. When your dog correctly touches the toy on command, no matter which toy is in which hand, you're ready to move on.

15. Sit on the floor with your dog sitting by your side.

16. Place both toys on the floor in front of you.

17. Send your dog to one toy, "Fido, Touch rope!"

 Down, Boy!

18. Praise and reward him when he goes to the correct toy.

Don't allow yourself to fall into a pattern as you send your dog to the toys. Dogs learn patterns very quickly.

19. Practice for a total of five repetitions, sending the dog to each of the toys.

You can add more toys the same way you did the second toy. Follow all of the training steps, even though your dog might appear to catch on much quicker. He probably is, but follow the training steps anyway. It's good training and will assure you that he is learning the new toy's name.

As you add a new toy, put the known toys away. Let him concentrate on the new one's name. Then when the new one is known, bring the first toys back out and reintroduce them. Emphasize the names of each of the toys, "Fido, Touch ORBEE™! Good boy!" and "Fido, Touch BALL! Good boy!"

Naming Your Things

Teaching your dog to understand the names of his toys is fun and potentially useful, especially when you want to play with him with a specific toy. However, when he knows the names of some of your things, he can then serve a useful purpose. How many times have you lost your keys? Or the television remote? When your dog knows the names of those items, he can help you search for them.

The list of things you can teach your dog to identify can be as long as you wish. Some ideas include the following:

- Your keys
- Your purse
- Your wallet
- Television remote
- Garage door opener
- Home phone
- Cell phone

You can also teach your dog to identify family members. Later in this chapter you'll learn how to teach your dog to search for items; when your dog knows family members' names, he can search for them, too.

Down, Boy!

If your dog likes to steal and hide things, don't teach him to identify anything of value to you. These dogs like to take advantage of this training.

Teach each item as you did the first ones. Follow the training steps, keep your training fun and exciting, and when each new item is learned, bring the old ones out for a reintroduction.

Playing the Name Game

The Name Game is a trick you can use to practice your dog's training (keeping him thinking). It's great for smart dogs who have a tendency to get into trouble if they aren't challenged regularly. You can also use this trick to show off to friends and family; after all, doesn't everyone need to see how smart your dog is? This is also great fun for therapy dogs. The game is easy to set up; you can take it to nursing homes, day-care centers, or hospitals.

The Name Game teaches your dog that everything is identified by a name.

Choose five different toys or objects. You can use just about anything, including the following:

- 🏠 Tennis ball
- 🏠 Squeaky toy
- 🏠 Rubber bone
- 🏠 Glove
- 🏠 Rolled-up sock

The idea is to have five items that look very different and have different-sounding names.

Teach your dog the name of each item as you taught him the names of his toys earlier in this chapter. Take your time, follow each of the training steps, and make sure your dog knows each of the items well.

If you will be asking your dog to perform this trick for a crowd or on therapy dog visits, you will want to use a lap tray as a table and place the items on the tray. Otherwise you can simply set the items on the floor.

To play the game, place all five items on the tray or on the floor. Ask a guest, friend, or family member to tell you which item to have your dog identify. This person will not give your dog the command (your dog might not work for that person and the person will not know the correct command or name of the item). For example, if the person said, "The leather glove," you can then tell your dog, "Fido, Touch glove."

> **BARK Troubleshooting**
> Some dogs are startled or worried by applause. Practice first at home and have family members applaud. If your dog is worried about it, see Chapter 14 and teach him that applause is a good thing and nothing to be frightened of.

When your dog Touches the glove, praise him and pop a treat in his mouth. Encourage your audience to applaud. Then ask someone else to choose the next item.

Teaching Your Dog to Search

Some dogs seem born knowing how to use their scenting abilities; others have to learn how to process information taken in through the nose. Some dogs, too, instinctively know how to follow scents. Terriers and hounds, for example, are much better following scents than many other breeds.

Any dog, of any size, breed, or body type can learn to find things by using his scenting ability. The dog who uses his nose naturally has an easier time than a dog who relies more on his sense of vision. *Brachycephalic* dogs (such as Pugs, bulldogs, Boston terriers, and French Bulldogs) are capable of learning these things but do sometimes have a more difficult time.

Dog Talk

Brachycephalic dogs have a shortened muzzle and convoluted nasal passages that often make breathing through the nose difficult.

Teaching your dog to search means teaching him to find something he cannot see and to use his nose to find that object. To begin, you need some treats that smell good to your dog, such as pieces of hot dog or dried liver. You also need a towel.

1. Sit on the floor with your dog. Let him smell the treat. Place the treat on the floor and quickly cover it with the towel.

2. Tell your dog, "Fido, Find the treat!"

3. If he immediately begins sniffing, praise him, "Fido, good boy! Good to Find It!" and lift the towel, letting him find and eat the treat. At this point in his training, reward the sniffing.

4. Repeat for a total of five successful repetitions and take a short break.

When your dog is actively sniffing and is trying to find the treat, let him work a little harder, delaying his reward until he gets closer to the treat. If he sniffs immediately over the treat, trying to sniff it through the towel, praise and reward him.

If your dog tries to stick his nose under the towel, lift the towel to let him succeed, then praise him even more, and add a few more treats to his reward. This is the behavior you want to get the strongest reward.

As your dog learns that you want him to find the treat hidden under the towel, you also want him to figure out how to get that treat. You don't want him to think the trick is to sniff and then wait for you to lift the towel, so encourage him to sniff and to nose the towel. If he tries to slide his nose under an edge of it, praise him!

Some dogs will actually pick up the towel in their teeth, moving it away from the treat. Let your dog figure out how to get it himself, just don't let him get too discouraged.

When your dog is finding the treat under the towel quickly, with little hesitation, begin hiding it in different locations. Sit on the floor with a towel, a shoe, and a small cardboard box, as well as some good treats.

> **Dog Talk**
> The command **Find** will always be combined with the name of an object (such as treat or ball).

> **BARK Troubleshooting**
> If your dog is easily discouraged or is too timid to try something new on his own, place the treat under an edge of the towel. Let him find it there, and then gradually move the treat toward the center of the towel, letting him find it on his own each time.

1. Place the towel, shoe, and box on the floor in front of you.

2. Turn your dog's head toward you and cover his eyes.

3. Drop the treat in one of the items (such as in the shoe) and then uncover your dog's eyes as you tell him, "Fido, Find the treat!"

4. Touch each of the items with a finger as you encourage him to sniff, "Find It! Good boy!"

5. When he finds the treat, praise him enthusiastically!

6. Do a total of five repetitions and take a short break and then try it again.

Over several training sessions, hide the treat in different objects. When your dog is doing this well, finding the treat each time, begin hiding the treat farther away from him.

7. Sit your dog with his back to the area where you will hide the treat. Or, if he keeps turning around, take him into another room and have him stay.

8. Hide the treat in an easy-to-find spot, such as on the sofa just under the edge of a throw pillow.

9. Bring your dog back into the room and tell him to Find the treat.

10. When he begins sniffing, praise him. When he moves toward the treat, praise some more. When he finds the treat, be enthusiastic, "Good boy! What a smart dog!"

11. Do a total of five repetitions and take a break.

BARK **Troubleshooting**

If your dog hesitates to move (he expects the treat to be close to him), walk with him toward some objects he can sniff. When he moves forward himself (perhaps when he smells the treat), praise him.

With practice, you should be able to hide a treat while your dog waits in another room, and then bring him back into the room and he'll find it without your help.

Combining It with Named Items

You can also teach your dog to find items that he knows the name of, such as his toys and the things of yours that you have named for him. You can teach these the same way you introduced the Find command except you will give him treats when he finds these items instead of him rewarding himself by eating the found treat.

1. Take one item, such as a tennis ball. Have your dog touch the ball, "Fido, Touch ball!" so you get his attention on the ball while at the same time refreshing him on the ball's name.

2. After five repetitions, take the ball and hide it under the towel. Tell him, "Fido, Find the ball!"

3. When he finds it, praise him, pop a treat in his mouth, and let him play with the ball.

4. Repeat for five repetitions and take a short break.

After the break, repeat the exercise, except hide the ball in different places. Help your dog search if you need to, but let him do it on his own as much as possible.

 Bet You Didn't Know

If a particular family member is always losing something (such as keys or the remote control), practice this trick often so your dog knows it well. Then when the item is lost, your dog can help that family member find it.

When he can find the ball when it's hidden, put it away and do the same thing with other items that your dog knows by name. This is not only fun, but it's challenging for him. He has to think, and that's always good. It's also a very handy skill. When you've lost your car keys, you can look for them but you can also use your dog's natural and learned abilities, "Fido, Find my keys!"

Finding Friends and Family

Your dog can learn people's names just as he did the names of things. Teaching the names of people is a little different than items, though, because it's tough to place them on the floor and have your dog touch them. However, you can teach your dog to recognize people by their names by playing a game.

1. Have one family member show your dog a treat. As you hold your dog, have the family member walk into another room. Let your dog watch the person (and treat) walk away from him.

2. When the person is in the other room, tell your dog, "Fido, Find Maggie!" (or whatever the person's name is) and let go of his collar.

3. If your dog followed Maggie to the other room, praise him. Maggie should give him the treat as soon as he reaches her. As you follow him, continue to praise him.

4. After a total of five repetitions, take a break.

5. After a break, repeat the steps but have Maggie go somewhere different each time.

6. Stop after five repetitions.

Gradually, with practice, make the searches harder. Maggie can hide in closets, behind the bed, or behind a door. Maggie should always offer a treat when she's been found and you should be following the dog, offering praise.

When your dog can find Maggie, begin all over again with another family member, "Fido, Find Bob!" Follow the same training steps.

> **BARK** **Troubleshooting**
>
> If your dog goes to Maggie when you're asking him to Find Bob, tell Maggie to ignore the dog. She should not react at all. You can ask Bob to call your dog and when he moves toward Bob, you should repeat the command to Find Bob.

The Find It Game

You will play the Find It Game by asking your dog to find something or someone who is hidden. When he finds what he's supposed to find, he gets praise and a great treat. The Find It Game can be played many ways. You can hide multiple items or you can ask a few people to hide. Either way your dog should find the item or person you name. If he finds something or someone other than the named item or person, he is not rewarded.

For example, you can ask three kids to hide themselves in the living room. Bob can hide behind the sofa, Jim can crawl under the coffee table, and Jane can pull the sofa throw over herself on the floor. Bring the dog in from another room and tell him, "Fido, Find Jim!" When he goes to Jane or Bob, he is ignored. When he goes to Jim, Jim will give him a treat and you'll praise him, pet him, and tell him what a smart dog he is!

The Hero Game

As a kid, I was amazed by Lassie; she could figure out Timmy was in trouble before he knew it, and then she could alert someone and bring them to Timmy before he was hurt. What an amazing dog! The people were amazing, too. They always knew that Lassie wasn't just barking but was trying to get someone to follow her.

You can make your dog a hero by teaching him to bark when he finds someone. Family members can learn that a Find by the dog followed by barking means "Fido says you're needed." For example, if it's dinner time, tell your dog, "Fido, Find Dad and Speak!" Fido will dash off, looking for Dad, and will bark as he's working. When Dad discovers a barking dog at his side, he knows that someone has sent the dog for him and he can come to dinner.

Your dog already knows the Name Game, and has been taught how to find someone, so all you need to do now is teach him to bark on command. This is really easy because most dogs love to bark.

1. Have a treat or toy your dog really likes.

2. Hold the treat or toy so your dog can see it and tease him with it. As you do, make some funny noises (hiss, or whistle, or click your tongue).

3. When your dog barks (or makes any noise at all), praise him, "Good to Speak!" and give him the treat or toy.

 Down, Boy!
Make sure you also teach your dog No Speak! when you want him to be quiet. You don't want your dog barking continuously or indiscriminately.

4. Repeat for a total of five repetitions and take a break.

As your dog gets bolder about making noise, wait and reward a good bark (rather than just a small noise) and emphasize the command Speak.

When your dog knows the command well, begin combining it with the search command and have the person being found tell your dog to speak when the dog finds him. Both of you can then praise the dog.

Teaching the ABCs

When your dog can recognize and touch the letters A, B, and C on command, you can use this trick to amaze your friends and family! No one thinks dogs can learn their letters; after all, only people can read. Right? Wrong!

At a craft store or hardware store, find wooden cut-out letters, such as the kind used to make signs. A, B, and C are fine, or you might want to choose letters that spell the dog's name. Rick Hawes, owner of Kelsey, a yellow Labrador Retriever, taught her to spell FEED ME.

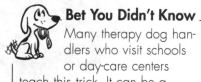

Bet You Didn't Know
Many therapy dog handlers who visit schools or day-care centers teach this trick. It can be a great motivator to encourage children to read!

1. Using one letter at a time, go through the same process that you did earlier in this chapter to name your dog's toys. (See "Naming the First Toy," earlier in this chapter.)

2. When your dog recognizes the first letter by name and is Touching it without hesitation, name the second letter. (See the section earlier in this chapter, "Naming Subsequent Toys.")

3. When two letters have been named, make sure your dog recognizes each letter's name.

4. Have A in one hand and treats in your other hand.

5. Ask your dog to touch A. When he does, praise him and pop a treat in his mouth.

Teach your dog to touch and identify one letter at a time.

6. Repeat for a total of five repetitions and take a short break.

7. Have B in hand and repeat steps 1 through 3.

8. Have A in one hand and B in the other. Have some treats in your pocket or close at hand.

9. Tell your dog to Touch A. If he does, praise him and pop a treat in his mouth.

10. If he Touches B instead, don't react at all. Just quietly wait. If he then Touches A, praise him. If he doesn't do anything, ask him again to Touch B.

Before you add a third letter, you want to make sure your dog really knows which shape is A and which shape is B. To make him think, repeat these training steps often. Sometimes hold A in your right hand and B in your left, and sometimes reverse them. As you practice, don't go back and forth, A, B, A, B, A. Instead, mix it up. Do B, B, A, B, A, A, A, B. Make sure your dog is listening and thinking.

Ask your dog to choose between two or more letters only when you believe he understands what you're asking him to do.

When your dog can Touch A or B on command, with very few problems, go back to the original training steps and add C.

Riker, my five-year-old Australian Shepherd, knows A, B, C, X, Y, Z, 1, 2, and 3. So here's a challenge: How many letters and numbers can you teach your dog?

Bet You Didn't Know

Craft stores also have wooden shape cutouts. You can teach this same trick using a heart, circle, square, diamond, or star.

The Least You Need to Know

🏠 Your dog can learn the names of a variety of things, from his toys to items you sometimes lose.

🏠 Teaching your dog to find lost items is very useful and well worth the time and effort it takes to teach it.

🏠 The Name Game and Find It Game are good training games and a wonderful way to show off.

🏠 Your dog can learn to recognize the letters A, B, and C. This is a great trick for therapy dogs.

Chapter 10

Retrieving More Than Toys

In This Chapter

- Teaching a vocabulary
- Making the retrieve exciting
- Retrieving by name
- Introducing scent discrimination

Teaching your dog to retrieve reliably introduces a whole new world. Not only can he retrieve toys for exercise, but he can retrieve items as part of a trick routine, he can find and bring back named items, and he can help you around the house. In Chapter 9, we taught your dog the names of many items and taught him to Find and Touch them; now we're going to combine the Retrieve with those skills so he can find your keys and bring them to you. Wow! Imagine the uses for that skill!

Perfecting the Retrieve

In Chapter 3, you learned how to introduce the Retrieve to both natural retrievers and those dogs who weren't especially excited about the Retrieve. The training steps taught in that chapter should have given your dog the basics of retrieving. If he is still not a strong retriever, go back to those steps and review them. Take as long as you need (a few days or even a couple of weeks) and make sure you and he are comfortable with the basic steps.

When your dog will eagerly chase after a ball and bring it back it you, dropping it in your hand or at your feet, then you can move on to the training steps outlined in this chapter.

Working on the Vocabulary

As with all of the tricks taught in this book, the commands can be made using any words you prefer. However, to keep things simple, I will teach the Retrieve using some commonly used commands.

- Get It! means go after the item to be retrieved and pick it up in your mouth.

- Bring It Here! means bring that item to me.

- Hold It! means Hold It in your mouth when you bring it to me; don't spit it out on the ground.

- Give means give it to me by dropping it in my hand or on my lap.

Retrieving is great fun, super exercise, and can also be the basis for many tricks.

Throughout the training in this chapter, these commands will be emphasized. All were taught in Chapter 3 except Hold It. To teach your dog this command go through the following steps:

1. As he brings a retrieved item back to you, encourage him to bring it close to you.

2. Before he can spit out the item, gently touch his lower jaw with your hand (pushing upward slightly) and tell him, "Fido, Hold It!"

3. As he Holds It without fighting you, praise him, "Good to Hold It!"

4. Have him wait just a second or two initially, then tell him, "Fido, Give!" and praise him as he releases the item.

As you practice the Retrieve over several training sessions, help him hold the item for a few seconds longer.

> **Troubleshooting**
>
> If he doesn't want to Hold the item and fights you to spit it out, don't wrestle with him or fight to make him Hold It. Instead, turn your back and walk away. Show him that if he won't Hold It, there will be no more retrieving games. When he does Hold It, you'll throw the toy again. He'll learn.

Before moving on in this chapter, make sure your dog knows and understands each of the vocabulary phrases. When he knows them well, there is less confusion when he's asked to retrieve a variety of items; the commands will remain the same, only the name of the item changes.

Keeping the Retrieve Exciting

The Retrieve is a great game that many dogs thoroughly enjoy. However, when the Retrieve is also used as a trick and as a help around the house, the dog might be doing a lot of them. That's okay if the dog is a natural retriever and has the desire to do it, but if he is not a natural retriever, and is doing it to please you, the Retrieve will turn into something less than fun.

You can keep the Retrieve fun by using the tug-of-war to spice it up every once in a while. If you see your dog begin to slow down or lose his spark, grab the rope toy and do a few tugs with him. Then throw the rope toy and tug it again when he brings it back. Just remember never to allow him to "win" the tug-of-war games (see Chapter 3).

Use your voice to keep the Retrieve fun, too. When you send your dog after the item, tell him "Fido, Get It! Good boy! Yeah!" in a happy tone of voice. When he grabs the item, say "Fido, Bring It Here! Good boy! Super!" and when he gives it to you, praise him some more.

You can also keep the Retrieve fun by varying the things he's asked to retrieve. If you're throwing the ball or toys for exercise, use different ones each play session or even swap toys midway through. You can even have three or four toys, and as he brings one back, toss out a different one. If you're using the Retrieve to help you, ask him to bring back an item of yours and then ask him to get a toy that he can play with. As the adage says, variety is the spice of life.

Bet You Didn't Know
Keep the Retrieve exciting by stopping before your dog gets tired. If you play too hard and too much, he might blame the game for his exhaustion and refuse to play anymore.

Retrieving by Name

In Chapter 9 your dog learned to identify several items by name, both his toys and some things of yours. In that chapter, though, we just wanted him to Touch those items, not Retrieve them. However, sometimes retrieving the item becomes a neat trick and can also be a help to you. So we're going to combine the skills from Chapter 9 with the Retrieve.

To begin, choose two toys your dog can identify by name very well. Refresh those names by doing some Touches with each item and then placing them side by side and asking your dog to touch each on command. When he can do it well, you're ready to move on.

1. Do a few play Retrieves with a tennis ball or other favorite retrieving toy to get your dog excited and in the mood to retrieve.

2. Sit your dog in the Heel position, holding the toy in your right hand as you hold your dog's collar with your left hand. (Let's use a porcupine squeaky toy as an example, calling it a porcupine.)

3. Show the porcupine to your dog. Tease him with it a little, shaking and squeaking it, and asking him, "Do you want this? Huh?" and toss it four to six feet away.

4. Tell him, "Fido, Get the porcupine!" and with your hand on his collar, give him a slight push forward toward the toy if he's a bit hesitant.

5. When he reaches the toy and picks it up, praise him, "Good boy to Get It!" and tell him, "Fido, Bring It Here!" Continue to praise him as he brings it to you.

6. When he reaches you, take it from him as you tell him to Give it to you. (Don't ask him to Hold It right now; we'll add that later.)

7. Praise him enthusiastically and repeat for a total of five repetitions.

8. Now place the second toy (let's say it's a ball) on the ground about six feet away.

9. With your dog sitting in the Heel position, hold his collar with your left hand and toss the porcupine toy with your right. Hopefully it will land two to three feet away from the ball.

10. Tell your dog, "Fido, Get the porcupine!" and let him go.

11. If he picks up the ball instead of the porcupine, take it from him, saying nothing, and have him Sit and Stay. Put the ball back where it originally was, and repeat steps 9 and 10.

12. When he does pick up the correct toy, praise him enthusiastically, telling him what a smart, wonderful dog he is!

After five repetitions, take a break. When you come back to train again, repeat the training steps using the ball as the active toy and the porcupine as the stationary toy. Your dog might be confused initially; after all, you just taught him to bring back the porcupine! However, he'll learn. Just follow the training steps.

Bet You Didn't Know

Some dogs get stressed when they are asked to think and make decisions. If your dog seems to want to avoid your trick-training sessions, or is panting or yawning, back off your training a little. Play more games and slow down the training steps. Concentrate on helping your dog succeed.

When your dog will retrieve the correct toy as it's tossed, you're ready to move on.

Your next goal will be to have both toys set out in front of your dog, with neither toy being thrown. Throwing the toy makes it a more exciting target; that's why we threw it in the beginning. However, by now your dog should know each toy's name, and the Retrieve command. So he's ready to do this.

13. Have your dog Sit in the Heel position. Tell him stay and walk away from him.

14. Place two toys (such as the porcupine and the ball) about six feet away and about two feet apart from each other.

15. Go back to your dog. Tell him to Retrieve one of the toys, "Fido, Get the porcupine!"

16. If he hesitates, urge him forward with a hand on his collar. You can even take a step forward if you need to. As he moves forward, encourage him.

17. When he picks up the correct toy, praise him enthusiastically, "Yeah! Good boy! What a smart dog!" And then call him back to you, "Bring It Here! Good boy!"

18. Tell him to Give the toy when he brings it back to you, praise him, and pop a treat in his mouth.

19. Repeat for a total of five repetitions and take a break. Repeat for the next three to four training sessions.

As you train, vary which toy you ask him to Retrieve and be careful you aren't establishing a pattern. Dogs catch on to patterns fast. So, for a five-repetition training session, you might send him to the ball twice in a row and the porcupine three times in a row.

When he's choosing the right toy ninety percent of the time, add a third known toy to the game. As with these toys, refresh his memory with a game of Touch, and then some plain retrieves with just this toy. Then add it to the Retrieve game with the other two known toys.

Troubleshooting

BARK If your dog is over-excited about retrieving and simply grabs the first toy he sees (not listening or even thinking about identifying the toy), practice this on leash so you can slow him down. If you need to, guide him.

When your dog is retrieving well, choosing the right toy on command, and is not showing any signs of stress, begin asking him to hold the toy before he gives it to you. As he brings it back, touch his lower jaw gently as you tell him, "Fido, Hold It." Wait just a second or two, and then tell him, "Give! Good boy!"

"Go Get the Newspaper!"

I am not a morning person; in the morning I am rumpled, often grumpy, and not at all neighborly. Because all our local newspapers are delivered early in the morning, I want to spare my neighbors the sight of me shuffling out to get them while I'm half awake. I just send Dax out for the papers. This has been her job for most of her life and I love it. I'm sure my neighbors appreciate it, too.

Getting the newspapers is not hard. The papers are easy for the dogs to pick up when they are fastened with string or rubber bands; even in the plastic bags they're fairly easy for them to grab. The larger Sunday papers can be wide and heavy, but Dax won't allow us to help her bring those in; it's her job and she wants to do it!

Before you teach this trick (or job!) make sure your dog is reliable off leash. You don't want to send him after the newspapers and have him take off down the street. He should have a reliable response to the Come command when off leash. If you're the least bit worried, have him on a long leash while you do this.

Play tug-of-war with a tightly rolled newspaper to build your dog's excitement and enthusiasm.

1. To begin, take a section of newspaper (maybe ten pages) and roll it tightly. Fasten it with a couple of rubber bands or some duct tape.

2. Play tug-of-war with this to get your dog excited about it, "What's this, huh? Get It! Yeah!"

3. When he will grab the rolled paper and play tug-of-war with it, ask him to Give it, and then toss it a few feet away, telling him, "Fido, Get the paper!"

4. When he goes after it, praise him and encourage him to bring it back. Have him Give it to you and praise him again.

5. Repeat this for a total of five repetitions and take a break. After a short break, repeat the training steps again.

> **Bet You Didn't Know**
>
> You can teach your dog the name of the newspaper by playing the Touch Game with him just as you did with his toys in Chapter 9.

Toss the newspaper a few feet away as you say, "Get the newspaper!"

Repeat this over several days. If your dog is excited about retrieving, he should pick this game up very fast. As he does, gradually increase the distance you toss the newspaper until you can throw it the length of your porch or driveway. Then stand where you would like to wait in the morning, and throw it to where the delivery person normally leaves it. Send your dog after it, praise him, and call him back.

When your dog is retrieving the thrown paper well, with no hesitation, take the next step of creating the actual morning scenario of the paper having been thrown without the dog's witnessing it. Leave your dog in the house and place the newspaper in the normal delivery spot outside. Go back in and send your dog for the paper. You might need to take a step or two forward with him, but if you have trained all the steps so far, he should go out after it eagerly. When he grabs the paper, praise him, "Yeah! Awesome job!"

When your dog will retrieve the newspaper, stop throwing it and instead begin placing it where it might normally be found.

After several training sessions over several days, begin varying the location of the paper so your dog learns to search for it. After all, the delivery person might have an off day and the paper could end up under your car or in the bushes; you want Fido to be able to find it wherever it's hidden.

"Get Your Leash!"

Many dogs learn this trick on their own, especially when the leash is normally kept in an easy-to-find location, such as on a coat rack. After all, dogs learn quickly that when the leash is hooked to their collar, they get to go for a walk!

If your dog hasn't taught himself this trick, it's an easy one to teach. First, decide where to hang the leash. It needs to be a knob or hanger that the leash can drape over without getting caught. You don't want your dog to grab the leash and pull a coat rack down on himself, or yank a hanger out of the wall. Then get in the habit of putting the leash there when you come in the house.

Roll up your dog's leash so it's about the size of a rolled-up newspaper. Fasten it with a couple of rubber bands. Now play some tug-of-war with it to get your dog excited, "Is this your leash? Get It! Yeah!" When he's excited, toss it a few feet away, "Get your leash! Good boy!" Repeat this, playing retrieving games with the leash as you've done with other items.

Bet You Didn't Know

Teach your dog the name of his leash by doing the Touch Game with him as you did with his toys in Chapter 9.

When your dog will retrieve his leash from across the room, unroll it. Now your dog has to deal with its length. Throw it for him, just a few feet away at first, then across the room, always encouraging him. He will have to figure out how to pick it up and how to hold it so he doesn't step on it and jerk it out of his mouth. Some dogs figure out how to fold it themselves and hold several lengths of it in their mouth; others learn to sidestep to avoid the leash. When your dog is comfortable with retrieving the unrolled leash, you're ready to move on in his training.

1. Have your dog Sit and Stay about halfway across the room from the place where you will be hanging the leash. Make sure he's facing that spot.

2. Walk away from him and hang the leash on the rack, making sure it will pull off easily.

3. Go back to your dog and send him for his leash, "Get your leash! Good boy!"

4. Be ready to step forward with him to help him should he hesitate.

5. As he gets to the leash, encourage him, "Get your leash! Yeah!"
as some dogs feel they will get into trouble if they pull something down or off a piece of furniture.

6. When he pulls it off the rack, go to him and praise him enthusiastically!

7. Repeat for a total of five repetitions and take a break. When
you come back, repeat all of these training steps.

When your dog is getting his leash with no hesitation, stop walking toward him and instead, ask him to bring the leash to you. Praise
him as he does, of course. After several days of this, you can ask him
to Hold the leash (instead of dropping it) for a few seconds before
you tell him to Give it to you.

When your dog will, on command, go across the room to get his
leash, pull it off the rack, bring it to you, and Hold It until you ask
for it, you can then begin sending him for his leash from another
room. As you do so, in the beginning, follow him to the doorway of
the room just to make sure he doesn't get distracted. But when he
has his leash, go back into the room where you started so he can
bring the leash all the way to you.

"Take This to Dad!"

Have you ever been involved in something—a project, washing the
dishes, or maybe even just comfortably reading a book—when a family member calls out and wants you to bring them something?
"Honey, will you bring me the screwdriver from the junk drawer?"
You want to help but also find it annoying. Well, let Fido help.

You will be combining several previously taught skills. First, go
back to Chapter 9 and review the section on teaching your dog to
realize that everything has a name, and make sure he knows your
family members' names.

Then, review the section in Chapter 9 on teaching your dog to search for those family members. Stage a few practice searches so your dog can find those people by name. When he can do that, you're ready to move on.

Earlier in this chapter, I taught you how to teach your dog to Hold an object until you told him to Give it to you. Practice this, too, until he will Hold objects for at least a minute and will wait for your command to Give it to you.

When your dog can do all three of these skills well, you're ready to continue.

1. Choose an object that is easy for your dog to carry, such as a rolled-up newspaper or one of his toys.

2. Have a family member sit across the room from you.

3. Hand your dog the newspaper, tell him to Hold It, and then say, "Fido, Find Dad! Take this to Dad!"

4. Dad should then quietly call your dog, "Fido, Bring It Here!"—quietly, to encourage him to come without getting him so excited he spits out the newspaper.

5. Dad should then praise the dog for coming and tell him to Give him the paper. You can then both praise him.

6. Repeat for a total of five repetitions and take a break. Come back later and repeat these training steps.

> **BARK) Troubleshooting**
> If your dog drops the item, simply pick it up, take your dog by the collar, go back to your starting point, and begin again. Don't scold or berate him. This takes concentration, so just help him do it correctly and praise him when he does.

After several days of practice, you can begin sending your dog farther away. The family member can be in the next room or down the hall. Very gradually, as your dog succeeds, ask him to search out family members with the rolled-up newspaper in his mouth.

When you can send your dog from one room and the dog will search the house for the named family member, you can then begin asking your dog to carry other items. He doesn't need to know the names of these items; after all, you'll be handing them to him. All he needs to do is hold and carry them.

You can teach your dog to carry ...

- Small tools, including screwdrivers and pliers.
- A book or magazine.
- A box of facial tissues.
- A roll of paper towels.
- A flashlight.
- A cordless phone or cell phone.
- The television remote control.

Some dogs hesitate to carry metal objects or things that feel funny in their mouth. You can get your dog over this easily. Smear some peanut butter on a metal spoon. Don't use a lot of peanut butter; you want your dog to lick the spoon thoroughly to get the treat and in the process get used to the metal. Hold the spoon while he licks it. When he's fine with this, put the spoon with the peanut butter on the floor and let him lick it, scooting it across the floor as he works at it. He will quickly learn that metal things can be the source of good stuff!

If you have items you would prefer not to be covered in dog slobber, you can teach your dog to carry a basket. Simply teach him the name of his basket, show him how to retrieve it (encouraging him to pick it up by the handle), and then tell him to Hold It. You can then place anything in the basket and have him carry it as he searches out the named family member. "Good dog!"

Teaching Scent Discrimination

Scent discrimination is an advanced obedience exercise, a great trick, and a useful tool. You will be teaching your dog to use his nose to find an object you have touched from among several that you have not touched. Your dog must use his scenting abilities (something that comes naturally to most dogs) combined with the Retrieve.

You need six cotton gloves; inexpensive gardening gloves are fine. Wash and dry them. When they're dry, use tongs to put five of them in a plastic bag. Close the bag. The sixth glove will be the one you touch on a regular basis. Before each training session, rub the glove between your hands or rub it on your forehead so it has a good dose of your scent.

Bet You Didn't Know
If you accidentally touch one of the gloves that is supposed to be unscented, wash it again using some bleach. The dog's scenting abilities are very good; if you foul the gloves he will make mistakes.

Bet You Didn't Know
Why use the food scent when you want him to recognize your scent? The dog's scenting abilities are excellent, but that doesn't mean he understands yet what we want him to do. By combining a scent he's attracted to (cheese or hot dog) with our scent, we make sure he is sniffing (inhaling) our scent.

1. Play a little tug-of-war with the glove. Toss it a few times and ask your dog to Retrieve it. Make the glove fun.

2. Now, put a tiny bit of hot dog or cheese (or another strong-smelling treat) inside the glove. Rub a little of the treat on the palm of your right hand.

3. Have your dog Sit in the Heel position and hold his collar with your left hand.

4. Toss the glove a few feet away. Cup your right hand gently in front of your dog's nose so he can smell the treat on your palm, then move your hand away as you tell him, "Fido, *Find Mine! Get It!*"

5. If your dog hesitates (perhaps looking at your hand with the scent on it), use your left hand to urge him toward the glove.

6. When he sniffs the glove, praise him, and encourage him to bring it to you.

Dog Talk
Find Mine means find the object with my scent on it.

7. Praise him again and give him a treat.

8. Repeat for a total of five repetitions and take a break.

Repeat this way for several training sessions or until the dog is going out to the glove eagerly and bringing it back with no hesitation.

This trick requires your dog to use his scenting abilities to find an object you have touched from among other objects you have not touched.

9. Now, using the tongs, take one of the unscented gloves and place it on the ground.

10. Sit your dog in the Heel position, tell him Stay, and place the scented glove (with a tiny treat inside) about six inches from the unscented glove.

11. Send your dog after you let him sniff your palm, telling him, "Fido, Find Mine!"

12. If he chooses the wrong glove, tell him to Give it and take it from him with the tongs, replace it on the ground, and take him back to the starting position. Repeat the steps, this time moving with your dog so you can encourage him to sniff the correct glove.

13. When he sniffs, praise him! When he picks up the correct glove, back away and encourage him to bring it with him. Complete the exercise and repeat it for a total of five repetitions.

BARK **Troubleshooting**

If your dog dashes out and grabs any glove, without sniffing, you can anchor the unscented gloves. If you're training outside, bend some stiff wire and force it into the ground so the gloves are held down. If you train inside, place the gloves on a piece of pegboard and use ties to hold them to the board.

Over several training sessions, vary the position of the glove with the scent. Sometimes have it on the right, sometimes on the left; place it in front of the unscented glove or farther away. When your dog will go out to the gloves, sniff them both, and choose the correct one, you're ready to move on.

Add one new unscented glove at a time, adding another when the dog is doing well and continuing to choose the correct glove. Eventually you should be able to have five unscented gloves on the ground with one scented one.

Then, begin decreasing the hot dog or cheese scent. For several training sessions, continue to have some scent on your palm but just a little; just touch the treat to your palm and then touch the treat to the glove, but do not put a treat inside the glove. When your dog is succeeding at this level, then stop touching your palm and the glove with treats; instead, just use your own body scent. Let your dog smell your palm and send him for the glove you have touched.

> **Bet You Didn't Know**
>
> When your dog will do this well with the cotton gloves, you can train with other items. Use six pieces of wooden dowel, six clean soda cans, or the professional obedience competition scent article, dumbbells.

The Least You Need to Know

- Perfect the skills learned in Chapter 9 before beginning to train the tricks in this chapter.

- The vocabulary for the Retrieve includes Get It, Bring It Here, Hold It, and Give.

- Sending your dog for his leash or for the newspaper are great tricks and useful skills.

- Scent discrimination is an advanced skill for obedience competition but is also a great trick.

Chapter **11**

Resisting Temptation

In This Chapter

- 🏠 Teaching the Leave It command
- 🏠 Learning to ignore food
- 🏠 Turning Leave It into tricks
- 🏠 Using temptation to build obedience

This chapter focuses on teaching your dog to ignore distractions. Although we touched on distractions in Chapter 3, that was a very basic introduction. Now we're going to challenge your dog's training, your ability as a trainer, and your dog's concentration. By teaching these skills, you will make your dog's obedience training more reliable as well as pave the way to some awe-inspiring tricks.

Teaching the Leave It

The *Leave It* command will help your dog ignore distractions that could get him into trouble. When he's not paying attention to you, he could miss your directions or commands, or could react inappropriately. He could also get into trouble by dashing into the street to chase a cat (running cats are big distractions!) or he could eat something that could hurt him (such as chicken bones or a poisoned rat).

Dog Talk

Leave It means ignore whatever it is you're paying attention to as I say it.

On a walk, he could react to the dog behind the fence, lunging and growling. The world is full of distractions—which is why they're called distractions!

1. Begin this trick with your dog on leash and a good-sized treat (such as a large dog biscuit) in hand.

2. Have your dog Sit in the Heel position. Hold the leash short and close to your dog but not tight. (Don't choke him!)

3. Show him the dog biscuit; even let him smell it.

4. Then tell him, "Fido, Leave It!" and drop the biscuit to the ground right in front of his front paws.

5. If he tries to grab it, use the leash to stop him and tell him, "No! Leave It!"

6. As he sits still, even if you're making him sit still, praise him, "Good boy to Leave It! Awesome!"

7. After a few seconds, put your hands on him, release him, and turn him away from the treat as you praise him, "Good boy!" (If you praise him with the treat at his paws, he's apt to reach down and grab it.)

8. After you turn him away and praise him, reach down and pick up the treat.

9. Repeat for a total of five repetitions and then take a break.

Practice these training steps until your dog is no longer trying to lunge for the biscuit and will hold the Sit nicely until you release him.

Bet You Didn't Know _____

The strongest distraction for a dog is food, especially foods that people might drop. We start training this trick with a dog biscuit because then if the dog does get it, it will not cause him harm—as, for example, a chocolate bar dropped by a child might. If the dog is very food motivated, the owner can begin this training with a toy.

The Leave It command is a very impressive trick with practical applications.

10. Have your dog Sit in the Heel position and hold a biscuit in your right hand.

11. Tell your dog, "Fido, Stay," then, "Fido, Leave It" as you drop the biscuit to the ground in front of him.

12. Take one step away while allowing the leash to hang loosely between your dog and your hand.

BARK

Troubleshooting

If, when you give your dog some slack in his leash, he begins lunging at the treat, use your voice and the leash to stop him, "No! Leave It!" Do not allow him to take advantage of the slack leash.

13. Wait a few seconds, then step back to your dog and praise him for Staying. Turn him away from the biscuit, praise him again, and reach back and pick up the biscuit.

14. Repeat for a total of five repetitions and take a break.

Practice these training steps for several days or even a couple of weeks. When your dog is holding his Sit Stay easily, with few mistakes, even with the treat on the ground in front of his paws, you can continue.

Now you want to teach your dog that Leave It applies to other things, not just a large dog biscuit. So go back to step 1 and repeat the training using other items as the distraction, including ...

- Half a peanut butter sandwich.
- A plate with a piece of leftover chicken on it.
- A chunk of cheese.
- Some appealing kids' toys.

When your dog will Sit and Stay with any distraction you place in front of him, you're ready to move on to the more difficult training.

Heel and Leave It

The Leave It command can be difficult for many dogs. But this exercise is relatively easy when the dog is Sitting and Staying; after all, the Sit and Stay is a control position. When learning the Sit and Stay, the dog learns he must control his impulses to move. However, ignoring distractions while walking is tough.

Before beginning this training, go back to Chapter 2 and review the Watch Me command.

1. To practice this, have your dog on a leash, and have some really good treats for a Watch Me. You will also need a dog bowl full of dog food or dog biscuits. Place the bowl on the ground.

2. Have your dog Sit in the Heel position ten to fifteen feet away from the bowl, facing it.

3. Tell your dog, "Fido, Watch Me! Heel" and walk toward the bowl. Concentrate on having your dog pay attention to you.

4. As you approach the bowl, if your dog looks at it or sniffs toward it, tell him, "Leave It!" and repeat your Watch Me command. Use your training treat to help him pay attention to you.

5. If he looks back to you when he hears the Watch Me command, praise him, "Yeah! Good boy!"

6. After you pass the bowl, stop and praise him and pop the treat in his mouth.

7. Repeat for a total of five repetitions and take a break.

 Troubleshooting
If your dog lunges toward the bowl, make an abrupt turn away from it (a right angle turn or an about turn) and take your dog with you. Have him Sit with his back to the bowl and ask him to Watch you. When he does, praise him.

Bet You Didn't Know
You can substitute other things as distractions, too. Ask some kids to play some active games where you're training your dog. Use your imagination.

Repeat these training steps for several training sessions. When your dog can ignore the bowl, move on to the next training steps.

8. Begin with your dog in a Sit in the Heel position, facing the bowl of treats about fifteen feet away.

9. Tell your dog, "Fido, Watch Me, Heel," and walk forward.

10. When you approach the bowl, tell your dog to Leave It if he looks or sniffs toward it. If he's focused on you and is ignoring the bowl, praise him enthusiastically!

11. Instead of walking past the bowl, this time turn and circle it. Walk around the bowl in a clockwise direction so your dog is on the outside of the circle. (You are between your dog and the bowl.)

12. After two circles, walk away a few steps, stop, Sit your dog, and praise him.

13. Repeat for a total of five repetitions and take a break.

Dogs who know Heel, Watch Me, and Leave It will have no trouble learning this trick.

Practice these training steps for two or three training sessions, and then change the direction of your circles so that your dog is walking on the inside of the circle, closest to the bowl. Watch for any lunges, but also readily praise good behavior.

> **Bet You Didn't Know**
> When your dog is heeling nicely and ignoring the bowl, set up two or three bowls, each with different treats. Walk a figure eight pattern around and between the bowls, challenging your dog to ignore them and watch you. Praise and treat him for his good work!

Coming Past Distractions

Many dogs can ignore distractions while Sitting and concentrating; and most can learn to focus on their owner and forget about distractions while Heeling. But ignoring distractions while running off leash is really hard. However, don't give up on your dog; many dogs can learn this, especially if you (as your dog's trainer) take your time, follow the training steps, and make sure your dog is doing each exercise well before moving on.

Before beginning this training, go back to Chapter 2 and review the Come command. Refresh your dog's training so he is eager and willing to Come when you call him.

You will need a long leash for this. A twenty- to thirty-foot length of cotton clothesline works well. A long cotton web training line is fine, too. (Appendix B lists a number of sources for training equipment.)

1. Have your dog on the long line and ask him to Sit and Stay.

2. As you walk away from him, place the bowl of dog biscuits on the ground in his path of travel to come to you when you call him.

3. Continue walking. When you're about twenty feet away from your dog, turn and face him. The bowl of treats should be easily visible.

4. Call your dog to Come, reeling the long line in as he runs toward you, and continue to praise him as he's running.

5. When he gets to you, have him Sit (so he doesn't turn around and dash back to the treats) and praise him.

6. Repeat for a total of five repetitions and take a break.

Practice these training steps for several training sessions. When your dog is running past the bowl without paying any attention to it at all, you're ready to move on.

Now it's time to up the ante. Add more distractions or better distractions. Go out and practice the Come while the neighborhood kids are playing football. Better yet, pack the kids a picnic lunch and practice the Come while they're eating on a blanket on the ground.

Don't try this off leash until your dog is very well trained and you positively know that he will do it correctly every time. He must also be mentally mature (two to three years of age). If you take the leash off too soon and your dog runs away from you, or gobbles down all the treats and then runs away, you will have a difficult time convincing him that he shouldn't do it. After all, the behavior is self-rewarding; he has fun when he runs and eats treats! So be careful.

Troubleshooting

If your dog is determined to get to the bowl of treats, use your voice to tell him sharply, "Leave It!" as he's sniffing it. Use the leash, too, to get him away from the treats. Hold the leash tightly and back away, pulling your dog with you.

Treats on the Paws

This trick will teach your dog to sit still while you place a treat or dog biscuit on each front paw. Your dog should continue to sit still without dislodging the treats and should ignore the treats until you give him permission to move and eat them. So, ultimately, your dog learns that sitting still and ignoring the treats is rewarded by eating them!

Make sure your dog is doing a very good Sit Stay, and his Leave It is good. A strong Watch Me can also help.

1. Have your dog Sit and Stay. Touch one of his front paws with your finger. Touch the top of the paw where you will eventually place the treat.

2. If he picks up that paw, tell him, "No, Stay!"

3. When that paw goes back down on the ground, praise him.

4. Touch that paw again. Praise him when he leaves it on the ground.

5. Repeat this for a total of five repetitions for each front paw. Take a break.

Do not go on to the next training steps until your dog is comfortable with having the tops of his front paws touched.

6. Have your dog Sit, tell him to Stay, and place a dog biscuit on one of his front paws.

7. If he looks at it, tell him, "Fido, Leave It. Watch Me. Good to Watch Me!"

8. Wait just a few seconds, praise him, and release him. Let him eat the treat off his paw.

9. Repeat this for a total of five repetitions and then take a break.

> **Troubleshooting**
> Some dogs are very sensitive to having their feet touched. Some are ticklish; others might have been injured. Some just are not used to it. Know your dog, and change your training to help him.

Practice these training steps for several sessions over a week or more. Don't go on to the next training steps until your dog is reliable with one treat on one paw. If he's lifting his paw, knocking the treat off, trying to eat the treat, or getting up from the Sit Stay, go back to the first training steps and begin again. Take it slow and make sure you're helping him succeed. Emphasize the basic commands Sit, Stay, and Watch Me. Your dog knows those commands, so use them.

When your dog is ready for the second treat on the second paw, go ahead and add it. This one is easy because he already knows what's expected of him. Praise him as you place the first treat on the first paw, and then add the second treat on the other paw. Keep the Stay time short and sweet so your dog can succeed, and then praise and release him.

Teach this trick only when your dog will do a solid
Sit Stay and understands the Leave It command very well.

Treat on the Nose

This trick can be tough to teach because many dogs have no concept of how their head is positioned. To keep the treat on top of the nose, the dog's head must be level. Most dogs do not hold their head exactly level. However, you can teach him.

1. Have your dog sit in front of you. You might want to sit in a chair and have his head over your lap.

2. Place one hand under your dog's chin to gently guide him, and at the same time, place a treat on the top of his nose.

Down, Boy!
This trick is really tough for short-muzzled dogs such as Pugs, Boston Terriers, and Bulldogs. It takes lots of practice to learn to balance on a short muzzle.

3. Praise him, "Good boy! Stay! Good boy!"

4. After a few seconds, release him, praise him, and let him flip the treat off his nose and eat it.

5. Repeat for a total of five repetitions and take a break.

6. Repeat these training steps for several days.

When your dog is holding his head steady, begin offering less guidance under his chin. When he can hold it on his own and your help is no longer needed, take your hand away and let him balance the treat himself.

BARK **Troubleshooting**
If your dog allows the treat to fall, tell him, "Fido, Leave It!" and pick up the treat. Do not allow him to eat a treat unless he completes the trick correctly.

As your dog learns this trick, and realizes that he gets the treat when he completes the trick correctly, he might begin to flip the treat in the air and grab it before it hits the ground. This is a great finish to the trick but is difficult to teach. Just reward your dog when he does flip the treat (rather than allow it to slide off his nose), "Good flip! Yeah! Good boy!"

This trick requires both concentration and balance
from the dog, as well as lots of self-control.

The Least You Need to Know

🏠 The Leave It command is an integral part of several tricks, is an important obedience command, and can help keep your dog safe.

🏠 Your dog can learn to ignore distraction while at a Sit Stay, Heeling, and Coming to you.

🏠 Teaching your dog to Sit with a treat on each paw requires several obedience commands as well as the Leave It.

🏠 Teaching your dog to balance a treat on the nose is hard, but most dogs can learn to do it.

Part 4

Showstoppers!

In this section, I introduce you to showstopping tricks that will amaze your friends and amuse your neighbors. I also show you how to put some of your dog's new skills to work so he can help you around the house.

Therapy dog work is a worthwhile volunteer activity that is in high demand. If your dog is a therapy dog or if you're interested in doing this in the future, I'll help you put together some tricks suitable for therapy dog visits.

For those who enjoy music and dancing, I introduce you to dancing with your dog. You can do this in the privacy of your home, or you can dance on therapy dog visits or even compete for titles and prizes in freestyle dancing competitions.

Chapter 12

Putting Your Trick Dog to Work

In This Chapter

- 🏠 Finding jobs for your dog
- 🏠 Getting you a bottle of water
- 🏠 Finding lost objects
- 🏠 Putting things away

Trick training is great fun; you know that. The process of training your dog is rewarding, especially when you see him master a difficult skill. Showing off your dog's skills is also enjoyable; after all, most people's dogs can barely walk nicely on a leash, and yours is capable of so much more!

But unless your dog is a therapy dog who visits various facilities every week, there is only so much showing off you can do. After all, you don't want people to run the other direction when they see you and your dog approach. But you can put this training to good use by teaching your dog to help you.

Thinking Up Jobs for Your Dog

The vast majority of dog breeds in existence today were bred to do a job. Australian Shepherds were designed to assist the shepherd or rancher; Rottweilers pulled wagons; Great Danes protected property. The list goes on and on.

Today many of these dogs are mainly pets. However, they still have the instincts to work. Many dogs get into trouble in the house and yard because they feel like they should be doing something, and they have nothing to do. When you give these dogs a job to do on a regular basis, they are thrilled, and very often problem behaviors decrease significantly.

Asking your dog to help around the house doesn't necessarily make things easier for you. After all, it would only take you a few minutes to pick up the damp towels on the bathroom floor and put them in the hamper. It will take twice as long to have your dog pick up one, carry it to the hamper, then go back for the other one and do the same thing. But sharing chores is always fun, and by teaching your dog to do it with you, you have the satisfaction of successful training, and of watching your dog take pleasure in doing something for you. Plus, you can always share with friends the fact that your dog picks up after your spouse!

Your Dog's Strengths

When deciding what types of jobs would be good for your dog, consider his strengths and abilities. If your dog had a hard time learning the Retrieve, don't focus on chores needing a good Retrieve. If your dog has a wonderful nose and likes to use it, teach him to find items you commonly lose.

Some questions to consider include the following:

🏠 Does your dog like to retrieve? He could find and bring back to you items you dropped or lost, and could bring things to you that you want, such as your slippers.

🏠 Does he use his scenting abilities a lot? Teach him to find things and people by name, and to take things to people.

🏠 Does he like to think? Does he learn easily? These dogs can be taught more complicated tasks, including turning lights on and off, and getting a bottle of water from the refrigerator.

🏠 Does he like to be close to you? These dogs should work with you instead of at a distance. Dogs who like to be close would be un-comfortable being sent away to do something.

 Down, Boy!
Be careful what you teach your dog. If he's too food motivated, don't teach him to open the refrigerator. If he has a hard mouth and likes to chew, don't have him retrieve delicate or expensive items.

By focusing on his strengths, you can make training much easier.

Your Needs

Granted, this training is for fun, but keep in mind everyone can use some help now and then. As I mentioned in earlier chapters, my dog, Dax, gets the newspapers every morning.

My five-year-old Aussie, Riker, knows how to brace himself to give me some support when I stand up from sitting or kneeling. I have a bad knee and sometimes it gets stiff. Riker will stiffen up, bracing himself, and take some of my weight on his shoulders. He holds that position until I'm up and no longer putting any weight on him.

Both Dax and Riker retrieve items for me, those I've dropped and those I've misplaced. Now, I am fully capable of bending over and picking these things up, and I don't lose nearly as many things as I send the dogs for; it's just fun to let them help!

So take a look around your house and yard, think about your daily routine, and decide where you could best incorporate your dog's efforts. Of course, think, too, about your training abilities.

Training your dog to help you could challenge your ability to train your dog, and that's good! You can both learn as you go along.

Getting a Named Item

This trick will teach your dog to bring a named household item to you. In Chapter 9, your dog learned to identify certain items by name, including his toys and some of your things, and he learned to find those things. Those skills are important here, so go back and review them. Your dog will also need the retrieving skills taught in Chapter 10.

Begin by having an item your dog is already familiar with at hand, preferably one that he learned the name of in Chapter 9, such as the cordless phone. Have some good treats in your pocket.

1. Have your dog Sit in the Heel position about two steps away from an end table or coffee table in your living or family room. The top of the table should be within your dog's easy reach.

2. Tell him to Stay and step away from him. Place the cordless phone on the end table or coffee table.

3. Go back to your dog and tell him, "Fido, Get the phone!"

4. If he immediately moves toward the phone, praise him.

> **BARK BARK Troubleshooting**
> The command taught in Chapter 10 for retrieving an item was Get It! If you use a different command (which is absolutely fine), you will need to use that command here. Don't change commands or you'll confuse your dog.

5. If he hesitates, use your left hand to move him from the Sit as you take a step forward. Praise him when he moves toward the phone.

6. When he picks up the phone, praise him and encourage him to bring it to you, "Good boy! Bring It here!"

7. Then tell him, "Fido, Give! Good boy!" and pop a treat in his mouth.

8. Repeat for a total of five repetitions, take a break, and come back and repeat these training steps again.

When your dog is stepping forward without your stepping forward with him and will pick up the phone off the table, bring it back to you, and give it to you, then begin farther back from the table. Let your dog walk three or four steps to the table, and then across the room. When he is doing this well, send him from outside the room (maybe in the hallway).

BARK

Troubleshooting

Dogs that have been taught to never touch anything on tables or furniture might be very hesitant at this stage of training. If your dog is, practice a few "Fido, Touch" exercises with the phone. Hold the phone close to the table, praise your dog enthusiastically, and then do another Touch with the phone on the table. Praise some more.

Teach this trick using an old phone that won't be damaged if your dog is too rough initially.

Then move the phone. Go through the previous training steps with the phone on another table in another room, then on a hassock, or on the sofa cushion. You need to practice with the same item in various places because dogs don't always generalize well. The first exercise taught your dog to Retrieve the phone from that specific table while he began the exercise in a particular spot. We varied his starting position because it then changed the exercise. We then changed the phone's position because that, too, changed the exercise. As he learns that the command is the same with all these variations, he can then make a generalization, "Ah ha! Get the phone means Get It no matter where it is and no matter where I am!"

"Get That, Please!"

After your dog is going to and picking up a named item, you can teach him to pick up an unnamed item. For example, you might have taught your dog to identify the cordless phone and your keys, but one day you drop your wallet. When your dog understands the command Get That, please, along with a pointed finger toward the item, he can pick up items he's not familiar with.

1. To begin, have an item that will be easy for your dog to pick up that is different from anything he's trained with so far. A wallet is good.

2. Place the wallet on the floor.

3. Walk your dog toward the wallet, point to it, almost touching it, and tell your dog, "Fido, Get That!"

4. If he reacts to the Retrieve command and picks up the wallet, praise him enthusiastically, take the wallet from him, and give him a jackpot of treats!

5. If he hesitates, as many dogs will do, flick the wallet with your pointed finger and encourage your dog to Get It.

6. When he does, praise him, take it quickly, and give him a treat.

7. Repeat for a total of five repetitions and take a break. Come back and repeat these training steps.

When your dog can pick up the wallet from the floor without any assistance from you, place it on the coffee table and work through the training steps again. Make sure you're still pointing at it with your finger close to the wallet. When he has no problem with picking up the wallet from the floor or table, begin moving it around and varying your dog's starting position.

BARK Troubleshooting

If your dog is hesitant, toss the item a few times (if it's not breakable). A moving object is always more fun than one that is still.

Then change the item. Remember, the wallet is an unnamed item to your dog, so choose another unnamed item. A roll of socks, a child's toy, or a screwdriver. The goal is to teach your dog to pick up the item you point at as you tell him, "Fido, Get That, please!"

When your dog will pick up anything you're pointing to, begin decreasing the hand signal. You want to continue to point at the object to be picked up, but not as closely as you have been. After all, if you're almost touching it with your finger, why not pick it up yourself? Begin to gradually increase the distance from the tip of your finger to the object you want your dog to pick up.

BARK Troubleshooting

If your dog is confused and doesn't understand what you want him to pick up, your hand signal isn't clear, or you have increased the distance from your hand signal to the object too quickly. Point to the object at a closer distance and see if that clears up the confusion.

Your ultimate goal with this exercise and the ones taught in Chapters 9 and 10 is to enable your dog to Find, Retrieve, or pick up any item you ask him to get, either named or unnamed.

People lose their keys all the time; when your dog can find them for you, you won't panic.

"Get Your Bowl!"

My five-month-old Australian Shepherd puppy, Bashir, already knows this trick. When I say, "Go Get your dish," he will dash away from me, even go to another room, find his dish, and bring it back. A potential side effect of this trick is that he will often bring me his dish even when I don't want it, and he has, on occasion, tried to bring me a full water dish. Such a helpful puppy!

Most dogs already adore their food dish, but some are leery of picking it up or moving it. You can get them over this by encouraging them to move it.

1. Take a spoonful of peanut butter and rub it on the inside of the empty food bowl.

2. Set the bowl on the floor and encourage your dog to lick the peanut butter. Identify the dish as you do so, "Bowl!"

3. Let him push the bowl all over the floor. He'll get used to the movement of the bowl and the sounds it makes.

4. Do this once a day (too much peanut butter is fattening, so don't do this more than once a day) for a few days.

5. Then run a tiny bit of peanut butter inside the bowl and some on the outer sides of the bowl. This will get your dog to move the bowl more, maybe even flip it.

6. Again, do this only once a day, but repeat it until the dog is easily moving the bowl and has no hesitation about the noise it makes.

7. When your dog is excited about his bowl, point to it and tell him, "Fido, Get That! Get your bowl!"

8. When he picks it up, praise him, "Yeah! Good job!" and take the dish from him, "Fido, Give." Praise him some more.

9. Repeat for a total of five repetitions and take a break.

10. At your next training session, tell him to Get his dish as you point to it, but begin decreasing your hand signal as he appears to understand the command.

11. Repeat for a total of five repetitions and take a break.

12. At your next training session, send him to his bowl, and when he picks it up, back away from him as you encourage him to bring it to you. Take it from him and praise him.

13. Repeat for a total of five repetitions and take a break.

As he learns this trick, you can begin sending him for his bowl from different places—down the hall, from another room. Just do so gradually and emphasize the praise.

Troubleshooting

If your dog does bring you his dish when you haven't asked for it, don't scold him. If you don't want him to do this unasked, just don't react, but definitely don't scold him.

"Pick Up Your Toys, Please"

My dogs have a wicker basket where their toys are kept. Like many well-loved dogs, they have quite a few toys. Although normally a few toys will be out of the basket, on some days the basket is empty and toys are scattered all over the living room floor, down the hall, into my home office, and even into the bedroom.

I can pick them up, of course, and often do. But it seems to me that if the dogs make the mess, they should clean it up, right? Well, you can teach your dog to pick up his toys, but he can't do it alone. You have to supervise and tell him to pick up each toy and then tell him to take it to the basket. But even though you need to direct the activity, it's still a great trick and fun for both you and your dog.

1. Stand next to your dog's toy basket. Begin by handing him a favorite toy.

2. When he takes the toy, praise him and tell him, "Basket," and point to the basket. He's used to following your hand signals and so will step to the basket.

3. Praise him and tell him to give you the toy, "Fido, Give." He's going to expect you to take the toy in your hand because that's what you've done for other retrieving tricks. Have your hand over the basket so that when he drops the toy, you let it drop into the basket.

4. Praise him, "Good Basket! Yeah!" and make a big fuss over him.

5. Repeat this for five repetitions and stop for a few minutes. Come back and repeat the training steps five more times.

Troubleshooting

You can use the Get That verbal command and hand signal (pointing) that you taught earlier in this chapter to direct your dog to the toys to be picked up. Or if your dog has learned the names of some of his toys (from Chapter 9), you can have him pick up those toys by name.

When your dog will willingly drop the toy into the basket and seems to understand the command, you can move on.

Your dog empties the toy basket; why shouldn't he clean up after himself?

Over several training sessions over many days, gradually ask your dog to pick up toys that are farther away and carry them to the basket. Continue to walk with him, encourage him, and direct him to drop the toys into the basket. But you'll find that your dog will figure this out. After practice, he will pick up the toy on your command and trot to the basket, but instead of waiting for you to tell him to drop it into the basket, he will do so on his own. Praise him, of course, enthusiastically! He's thinking now, not just waiting for your direction.

Eventually you might be able to sit on the sofa, drinking your tea, and tell your dog to pick up his toys and put them in his basket. But only a few dogs can do it this way; most dogs require more direct assistance.

Picking Up Other Stuff

You can use the skills for picking up toys in other ways.

- 🏠 He can pick up the damp towels off the bathroom floor and put them in the hamper.

- 🏠 He can put dropped trash in the trashcan.

- 🏠 He can help you put away the kids' toys.

- 🏠 He can drop a letter in a mailbox.

Just use the training steps outlined previously with a vocabulary for that particular activity.

Retrieving from the Refrigerator

This is a pretty complicated trick with several parts. The ultimate goal is to teach your dog to open the refrigerator door, get out a bottle of water, close the door, and bring the water to you.

Down, Boy!

Think about your dog's personality before teaching this trick. Don't teach it to dogs who might be prone to taking advantage of it! I can think of several dogs who would clean out the refrigerator in a heartbeat if they knew how to open the door!

Retrieving the Water Bottle

This is the easiest part of this trick. Your dog knows how to retrieve and has been introduced to a variety of objects, both to touch and to get for you. Adding a water bottle will be no trouble at all.

1. Start by getting your dog excited about the water bottle so you can teach him a name for it. Tell him, "Fido, Touch water bottle," and hold it up for him to Touch.

2. Praise him and pop a treat in his mouth.

3. Repeat for a total of five repetitions and take a break.

4. At your next training session, repeat the five Touch exercises and then instead of taking a break, gently toss the water bottle a few feet away.

5. Tell your dog to get it, "Fido, Get the water bottle!" and when he does, praise him.

6. Encourage him to bring it back to you and to Give it to you.

7. Repeat five times and take a break.

8. Practice these training steps several times over several training sessions.

When your dog is enthusiastic about retrieving the water bottle and will bring it back to your hand when you're standing about six feet away, you're ready to move on to the next training steps.

9. Prop open the refrigerator door. Clear off an area of a bottom shelf, making sure there are no meats, cheeses, or leftovers that might distract him or lead him to temptation! Place the water bottle on the clear spot on the shelf.

10. Stand in the open door of the refrigerator, point to the water bottle, and tell your dog, "Fido, Get the water bottle."

11. If he hesitates, verbally encourage him and touch the water bottle with the hand that's pointing to it.

12. When your dog touches the bottle, even if he just touches it with his nose, praise him! This is new territory here, so give him as much help as he needs.

13. If he takes the bottle in his mouth, praise him enthusiastically, tell him, "Fido, Give!" and pop several treats in his mouth.

14. Repeat for a total of five repetitions and take a break.

At your next several training sessions, repeat steps 9 through 13, keeping the excitement level high. As your dog's confidence grows,

Down, Boy!

I teach this trick with a plastic water bottle because it's much safer than other drink containers. Glass can break and can cut the dog's mouth if he bites down.

back away from him after he picks up the bottle, asking him to carry it to you.

When your dog will walk up to the open refrigerator, take the bottle in his mouth, and walk a few steps to give it to you, you're ready to continue to the next training steps.

Opening the Door

Opening the refrigerator door is the key to this trick; after all, if the door is closed and your dog can't open it, the trick is over before it's begun.

Go through your old towels and choose one to sacrifice. It can be a dish towel or bath towel but needs to be able to fit through the handle on your refrigerator.

1. Play tug-of-war with your dog with this towel, making a great game of it, "Fido, Get it! Yeah!" As you're playing, begin adding the word *Pull* while your dog is pulling hard on the towel.

2. Do this several times each day for several days. You can move on to the next training steps when you can hand your dog one end of the towel, tell him, "Fido, Pull," and he pulls.

Troubleshooting

If your dog is startled by the door opening when he pulls on the towel, add another training step. Encourage him to be close to you, open the door, and pop a treat in his mouth. Repeat this until he's over his discomfort.

3. Drape the towel through the handle of your refrigerator. Use a cable tie or something similar to fasten the towel so your dog can't pull it out of the handle.

4. With the refrigerator door slightly open (so the seal is not tight), offer the end of the towel to your dog, "Fido, Pull!"

5. When he takes the towel in his mouth, praise him! When he pulls on the towel and moves the door, praise him even more!

6. Repeat for a total of five repetitions, take a break, then repeat steps 4 and 5.

You can move on to the next training steps when your dog will pull on the towel, making the door open further, and is not startled about the door moving.

7. Most refrigerators have a tight seal, so opening the door takes quite a pull. You are going to have to encourage your dog to pull hard to break that seal but then to stop pulling after the door is open. With the refrigerator door shut all the way, tell your dog, "Fido, Pull!" and encourage him to grab the towel. When he Pulls, praise him.

8. If he opens the door himself, praise him well and tell him to let go of the towel, "Fido, Give," and pop a treat in his mouth.

9. Repeat for a total of five repetitions and take a break.

Closing the Door

Most people think closing the door is the most difficult part of this trick, but it really isn't. Go back to Chapter 1 and reread the section on touching a target. You will teach your dog to touch a target and then will put that target on the refrigerator door.

1. The target can be anything that can be put on the door; a sticker works well. Choose a sticker that is at least as big as the palm of your hand. Don't put it on the refrigerator yet.

2. Hold the sticker in your hand and tell your dog, "Fido, Touch!" and pop a treat in his mouth when he does.

3. Repeat for a total of five repetitions, take a break, then do it again.

4. Now you will add the command for closing the door, "Fido, Close," for example. Have your dog touch the sticker in your hand by saying, "Fido, Touch, Close the door!" and pop a treat in his mouth. He's not closing anything, but you're building an association between those words and Touching the sticker.

5. Repeat for a total of five times and then take a break. Come back, do it all again, and take another break.

6. Hold your hand with the sticker in your palm in front of the refrigerator door, do five touches, take a break, come back and do five more. Make sure you're continuing to use the entire command, "Fido, Touch, Close the door!"

7. Unpeel the sticker and stick it to the refrigerator door at your dog's nose height on the front of the door toward the side where the handle is. Your dog should be able to Touch the door and have it close.

8. Now do five Touches on the sticker, praise and treat your dog, take a break, and do five more. Use the entire command, "Fido, Touch, Close the door!"

9. After another break, do five more Touches to the sticker, but this time use the command, "Fido, Close the door!" Praise him and pop a treat in his mouth each time.

10. Open the door slightly (just a few inches) and have your dog Touch the sticker, using the Close command, and let the door go when he Touches it so that the door closes. Praise your dog enthusiastically and pop a treat in his mouth.

11. Repeat for a total of five repetitions, take a break, and do five more.

Putting It All Together

Review all of the parts of this trick before you put it all together:

🏠 Have your dog retrieve the water bottle a few times. First from a short tossed retrieve, then place it on the floor, and then from the shelf in the refrigerator.

🏠 Do a few easy tug-of-war tugs, then refresh your dog's Pull on the towel on the refrigerator.

🏠 Last but not least, do a few Touches on the sticker on the refrigerator door.

When your dog will do all of these, you're ready to put it together.

1. Walk up to the refrigerator, tell your dog, "Fido, Get me a bottle of water." If he dashes up to the refrigerator, praise him, "Yeah! Good boy!"

2. Tell him to Pull, praise him when he does, and when the door is open, tell him to Give so he drops it.

3. Right away (so the door doesn't close on him) tell him, "Fido, Get the water bottle."

4. When he grabs it, praise him, tell him to Hold It, and then tell him to Close the door. When he does, praise him enthusiastically!

It will take time and practice before you can sit in the living room in front of the television and send your dog to the refrigerator for a cold beverage. But with practice, your dog can do it.

Troubleshooting

BARK Your dog might drop the water bottle to close the door; he might not know he can do two things at once. Just keep having him pick up the water and then repeat the Close command. When it all comes together, give him a jackpot of rewards!

Turning Lights On (and Off)

Teaching your dog to flip a light switch isn't hard as long as he is tall enough to reach those switches when he stands on his rear legs. Many service dogs are taught this behavior because it can save a disabled owner effort and steps; for you, it's fun and it can come in handy.

This trick is best taught using a target, much like you learned target training in the refrigerator trick. However, this time the dog will touch the target with his paw instead of his nose.

Down, Boy!

Rough paws and sharp claws can damage switches, switch plate covers, and the surrounding wallboard. You might want to protect those surfaces before you begin teaching this trick.

Your dog will need to know how to shake paws before beginning this trick, so go back to Chapter 5 and teach (or refresh) the Shake. When he will Shake on command, offering his paw, you can move on to the next training steps.

1. Have a switch plate cover in your hand. A distinctive decorative one is nice because it will stand out to your dog.

2. Tell your dog, "Fido, Shake," and have him Shake by touching the switch plate cover in your hand.

3. Praise him, repeat for a total of five repetitions, and take a break.

4. Repeat the training steps above, but use the command, "Fido, Shake, Lights!" He knows the Shake command requires the use of his paw, and the word *Lights* is the word we'll use for this trick.

5. Praise him, of course, as soon as he touches the plate cover in your hand.

6. Repeat for five repetitions and take a break.

7. After several training sessions, begin decreasing the use of *Shake*, emphasizing the word Lights. When your dog will offer to paw the plate cover on the command Lights, you're ready to move on.

8. Begin the next training session near the wall where you will be having your dog turn the lights on or off.

9. Hold the switch plate cover close to the wall but at the same height you have been shaking hands with your dog.

10. Have him touch his paw to the plate five times, reward him well, and take a break.

11. The next training session, hold the plate several inches higher, have him touch it with his paw, reward him, and do five repetitions.

BARK Troubleshooting

Don't hesitate to encourage your dog to lift himself up. You can pat the wall, use a happy tone of voice, or even bounce a little yourself.

Gradually, over several training sessions over a couple of weeks, ask him to raise his paw higher and higher, until he's standing on his rear legs and touching the plate cover at the height where it is normally located.

When he will touch the switch plate cover easily at the normal height, begin having him touch the one fastened to the wall. Obviously, it should look just like the one he's been training with. At this point, too, you can keep repeating the Lights command until he paws the plate, thereby triggering the switch. Give him a jackpot of praise!

The Least You Need to Know

- Finding jobs for your dog is not hard; just look to his strengths and skills.

- You can teach your dog to get his dish and put away his toys.

- Your dog can learn to open the refrigerator, get you a bottle of water, and close the door behind him.

- Turning lights on and off is easy if your dog is tall enough.

Chapter **13**

Amaze Your Friends and Amuse Your Neighbors

In This Chapter

- 🏠 Putting a costume on your dog
- 🏠 Creating a routine
- 🏠 Building sets for a routine
- 🏠 Choreographing a show

Have you ever thought about putting one of your kids' Halloween costumes on your dog? Did some of the fancy bandannas at the local craft store call to you? Last Christmas, did you try to coax your dog into wearing reindeer antlers? If so, you're not alone! Costumes for dogs are big business, and the pet supply stores, dog supply catalogs, and online supply outlets offer a wide selection. Halloween is a huge time of year, of course, but accessories are also available at other holidays, especially Easter, Christmas, and the Fourth of July.

In this chapter we'll take a look at costumes for canines, and I'll show you how to create a routine by stringing several tricks together. If you put together a routine, you might decide to go all the way and choreograph a show using the tricks your dog has learned, plus

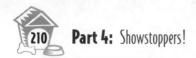

some sets and costumes. There's a lot involved in a show, but you and your dog will have a blast doing it.

Costumes Are Creative

I have an assortment of bandannas for my dogs for holidays throughout the year. On patriotic holidays, they wear red, white, and blue; at Christmas they have holiday bandannas; and at New Year's they wear shooting stars. Usually, they wear these to therapy dog visits and to my dog training classes, but occasionally they will wear them on walks or other outings.

I have found that something as simple as a bandanna can make people smile. People who might not normally like dogs, as well as people having a bad day, will smile, laugh, and reach out to pet a dog wearing a bandanna.

One of our trainers at Kindred Spirits, Katy Silva, has a Rottweiler named Sasha. Sasha is a big Rottie with a wide chest and a broad head. Even though she is a warm, loving therapy dog, some people are worried about her, because of both her breed and her size. So Sasha often wears colorful bandannas and simple costumes. It's hard to think a dog is dangerous when she's wearing bunny rabbit ears!

A friend of mine doesn't think dogs should wear clothes or costumes of any kind. He thinks they demean dogs. I understand his thinking; clothing and costumes should not be made to embarrass our dogs. But when used with a good heart, costumes can enhance what you do with your dog, from therapy dog visits to trick routines or even shows. If you like to dance with your dog, such as in the sport of freestyle (see Chapter 15), costumes are very much a part of the

 **Bet You Didn't Know**

You can make bandannas for your dog from scrap cloth. Find some scraps in your craft leftovers or at your local craft or sewing store. Fold a square in half, drape it around your dog, and decide on the right size. Trim it to fit and hem the edges. That's it!

act. When introduced correctly, most dogs enjoy wearing something that makes them the center of attention.

Creating Costumes

Costumes can range from kids' costumes adapted to dogs to commercially created costumes for dogs or even homemade or sewn costumes. A decorative outfit for your dog can be as simple or as elaborate as you want to make it.

If you decide to adapt a child's costume into a dog's costume, get a larger size than you would think you'd need. A fifty-pound child and a fifty-pound dog have entirely different proportions; a child's costume of that size would be very restrictive and binding on the dog—depending, of course, on the costume. If the costume was extremely loose and wide (such as that of a pumpkin) it might still fit.

Children stand upright, and most children's costumes build in some leeway for height so that one costume might fit children of different heights and ages. Dogs have long bodies, usually longer than a child of the same weight, and the rear legs are proportionately wider, especially in the hips. Plus the dogs' forelegs don't necessarily correspond with the way a child's arms might move.

 Bet You Didn't Know

A dog's chest is proportioned entirely differently from a child's. A child's chest is wide across (from arm to arm) and not very deep (from sternum to point of the shoulder). Dogs have deeper chests that are not very wide.

When you add in the fact that most kids' costumes have their decorations on the front (which would be under the dog's belly), it would seem that converting a costume would be a lost cause, but that's not necessarily so. Many kids' costumes can be made over for dogs.

A costume can be simple or elaborate; just make sure your dog is comfortable wearing it.

Take a look at the costume itself. How is it designed? If it's one piece, you have less leeway for conversions; two-piece outfits are easier. But even one-piece costumes can be used if the design will allow you to fit it. Can you make discrete slits in the costume? A slit at each leg could give your dog room to move. Or can you make it into two pieces by separating the top from the bottom, perhaps at the waist? Sometimes you can add more room over the hips and shoulders by inserting pieces of fabric at those points.

Down, Boy!

A dog's costume must not restrict freedom of movement. The dog's head, four legs, and tail should be able to move easily.

Some kids' costumes can be worn backward by the dog, so the decorated part is on the dog's back where it's visible. Again, depending upon the design, you might need to make some changes to get it to fit like this.

Costumes specifically made for dogs are obviously much easier to fit because they're designed for a dog's shape. The manufacturers usually provide guidelines as to how to fit these costumes; many require measurements of the chest and waist as well as the dog's body length. If you can find these costumes at your local pet supply store, bring your dog with you and try the costumes on him. If you have to order via catalog or Internet, call a customer service representative and find out how to measure your dog.

If you like to sew or do craft projects, dog costumes can be as simple or as elaborate as you like. For example, here is how I made one for my Australian Shepherd, Dax:

- At a discount store, I got a black child's T-shirt that fit her. I chose one made of a stretchy material so she could move without the shirt sagging.

- While doing Halloween shopping, I got a witch's hat with a big pointy tip.

- At a craft store, I got some gold glitter glue, two yards of clingy, filmy black material, and two yards of half-inch-wide elastic.

- I measured Dax's back from the point of her shoulder to the tip of her hips.

- I cut the material into a long length as wide as that measurement.

- I gathered one long side of the material and stitched it so it kept that gather.

- I used some of the elastic to make a tie to fasten around Dax's neck and sewed that to the gathered material, leaving several inches on either side of the material as ties.

- When draped over Dax, the gathers were around her neck, and the witch's cloak fell down her back and over each side.

- I trimmed the sides so that they fell almost to the floor but not quite so she wouldn't step on it.

- I then took a piece of elastic and fastened it to the hat so it would stay on the back of Dax's head (actually more on the top of her neck).

- Taking the outfit off, I then used the gold glitter glue and decorated the cloak and hat.

With the black T-shirt underneath, she looked every inch the glamorous witch!

With homemade costumes, you are limited solely by your imagination!

Introducing a Costume

Introduce a costume slowly, especially if your dog has never worn one before. Use the training tools you have learned teaching your dog tricks. For example:

1. Put a small piece of the costume on him.

2. Praise him as soon as it touches him.

3. Pop a treat in his mouth.

4. Immediately take the costume off of him and tell him what a wonderful dog he is!

5. Repeat for a total of five repetitions and take a break.

> **Bet You Didn't Know**
>
> After your dog has learned to wear a costume, and has been rewarded by the attention it generates, introducing each subsequent costume is easier.

The costume piece might have only been on him a second, but that's okay. He will learn to associate the costume with praise and treats. Gradually, over several training sessions over many days, you can introduce the entire costume. The more elaborate the costume and the more hesitant your dog, the longer you need to take introducing it.

It's easy to get excited about a costume for your dog, but don't let that excitement overrule your common sense. Take your time introducing it, and let your dog get used to wearing the individual parts of it before you put it all together. When he can wear the entire costume at home, and will move around in it, practice his obedience commands while he's wearing it. Then ask him to do some tricks. Only then should you start taking him away from the house while wearing it.

*Give your dog plenty of time to get used to the costume before taking him
away from home wearing it.*

Think Safety

Costumes can be attractive, make people laugh, and be a great addition to your trick training, but make sure each costume you ask your
dog to wear is safe.

- The costume should be easy to put on your dog. You don't
  want to have to force him into contortions to get it on.

- The costume should be even easier to take off. If he gets tan-
  gled or panics, it should come off easily.

- The costume should allow for easy movement of his head, all
  four legs, and tail.

- The costume should not block his vision.

- Your dog needs to be able to breathe freely through his mouth
  and nose.

There are a few other things to think about. Can your dog relieve himself while wearing the costume? This is a fact of life, and if he's going to be wearing it for a couple of hours, he might need to go. Plus, will he need to wear a leash and collar, and if so, how will the costume affect that?

Putting Together a Routine

Trick training by itself is fun; it adds spice to your regular obedience training, it enhances your training skills, and you and your dog enjoy the time spent doing it. If your dog is also a therapy dog, you can make people laugh just by having him do a few tricks.

But trick training can be elevated to a whole new level when you put several tricks together to create a routine. Girl, a Dalmatian owned by Marta Zarrella of Poway, California, is an unofficial mascot for a local fire department. Marta did some trick training with Girl and decided to teach her the fire department's lesson for kids, "Stop, drop, and roll"—that is, stop running, drop to the ground, and roll to put out the flames. Marta can then, during lessons with the kids, have Girl demonstrate.

Teaching this is not hard. Begin by teaching all three parts of it separately: the Stand, the Lie Down, and the Roll Over. Stand and Lie Down are obedience commands, and Roll Over is the trick. When the dog can do each by itself, you can then ask him to do them consecutively.

Putting together a routine just takes imagination. You also need to think about where you would use this routine.

- Day-care centers: Fun, simple trick routines are good, as kids are easily impressed and won't appreciate complicated training routines. Routines with lessons (such as stop, drop, and roll) are also good.

🏠 Kids' groups: If the group (such as Girl Scouts or Boy Scouts) is studying something specific, you could train with that in mind. Teach your dog to kick dirt over a campfire (fake, of course) or to follow bread crumbs back to a campsite.

🏠 Schools: This depends upon the age and the class. Classes studying behavior might be able to follow more complicated routines.

🏠 Nursing homes: Trick routines that make people laugh are great here. You can also have your dog offer people a tissue or a magazine, or other useful tricks and behaviors.

🏠 Hospitals: Most routines here should be quieter and circumspect, although laughter is too often in short supply.

Trick routines can also be great at local dog or pet events. Many pet supply stores host events with trick contests. Dog organizations, especially dog sports clubs and rescue groups, sponsor events with fun contests. Competing and showing off your dog's skills are fun no matter what the prize. A good routine that flows from one trick to the other will grab the audiences' attention and probably the judges', too!

Practice trick training at home with the costume before trying it away from home wearing it. The costume is, by itself, a major distraction for your dog.

Creating Sets

Sets (or stage props) are not necessary for most tricks and trick routines but they can add another dimension to both. Sets can be as simple as a few props and a backdrop (such as an old sheet) or as elaborate as a stage with props, furniture, a background, and sound effects.

At the graduation for one of our trick-training classes, a dog owner put together a simple trick routine with an elaborate yet portable set. Her dog, a Basset Hound named Hero, was the star. Hero, as befits his name, was going to save the damsel in distress, a toy stuffed Basset Hound. To save her, Hero had to climb the tallest mountain (a plastic child's slide with a ladder), swim the deepest sea (wade through a child's wading pool with six inches of water), and charge through the thickest forest (weave through a set of weave poles). When he completed all these challenges, the damsel was waiting for him in the tallest tower of the castle (on the top shelf of a small step stool). Obviously, with the narration explaining his challenges, the audience was enthusiastic and rooting for Hero. The sets were easy to put together and transport and easy for the dog to work with.

If you're creative, more elaborate sets can be built, painted, and decorated. Just keep in mind, your audience is always going to be more interested in what your dog is doing than in how elaborate your sets are.

Putting On a Show

A trick-training routine is several tricks performed one after another and may or may not have a storyline. This is great, but it isn't a show. A show has a storyline, a plot with a beginning and an end (such as Hero and the damsel in distress), and usually includes costumes and a set (although nothing needs to be elaborate).

If you decide to put together a show, either for family and friends, for a therapy dog visit, or for a special event, preparation is the key. Begin training far enough in advance so that your dog can learn his routine, get to know any props you might decide to use, and so that he can practice on the set.

A trick training show will have several parts:

- The tricks themselves

- A trick routine (which trick is performed first and the order in which the others are performed)

- Any props (leash, treats, costumes, and so forth)

- A set or background

- The narration and story

A show consists of a trick routine, costumes, props, and a story told through the tricks and narration.

So think about a story you could illustrate with your dog's tricks. You might even decide to make up a few new tricks. Then put together a simple set, a costume for your dog (and perhaps even for yourself), and decide on the narration. If you will be assisting your dog with his tricks, choose someone else for the narration. Make sure he or she can do the narration without laughing too hard!

You will also want to decide or find out where the show will take place. You might need to get your dog used to working on slippery floors, or on a stage, and might need to introduce him to other things that are new. If this is being held on a stage, has he ever seen a curtain being pulled back? Has he ever performed for an audience? What does he do when people clap or whistle?

One of my dogs years ago, Watachie, decided he really liked applause. We had been living in Southern California where dog shows were held outside. We trained and competed outside and Watachie was very successful. Then we moved to the East Coast where many of the dog shows and events were held in gyms or auditoriums. At one of our first dog shows there, a crowd was watching Watachie perform the obedience utility exercises (advanced level obedience). As he finished each exercise the crowd clapped and Watachie listened. He finally decided it was for him and when they applauded, he would turn, look, pose and smile, tongue hanging out. Of course, the crowd loved that, too, and clapped some more!

Bet You Didn't Know

Many nursing homes or special care facilities have regular shows or entertainment for their residents. They might welcome a show demonstrating some special tricks, especially if it fits in with the other entertainment.

Not all dogs like applause; some are worried about it. So if you decide to do a show, make sure you practice his tricks with family members applauding, whistling, and cheering him on.

Putting on a show is a great showcase for your dog's skills; just plan and train for it. Deciding at the last minute to do something like this rarely works. Your dog will be uncomfortable or maybe even frightened and your training will have been in vain.

One Show, Multiple Dogs

Just as a one-man or one-woman show on Broadway can be fascinating, so can a one-dog show. But an ensemble cast can entertain you for hours. Not only that, but an ensemble cast can cover up mistakes should one of the dogs be having a bad day!

Multiple-dog routines or shows do require more training. The dogs must be able to work together with no animosity, and without being distracted by one another. Prior planning and training is very important with multiple-dog casts. But it's worth it when it all comes together.

One Owner and Multiple Dogs

Dog owners who own more than one dog can design trick routines or shows that use all the dogs, and find niches in the routine for each dog's strengths. For example, with my three, Dax is the serious one; she can learn things quickly and is very reliable. Riker is quite athletic, thinks the world is great fun, and performs with enthusiasm. Bashir is still young but already loves to jump and retrieve, so I'll be sure to use those skills in his future trick training.

In addition to working with your dogs' strengths, you can also find a few tricks that both or all of your dogs can do. A spin done in unison is very nice, as are jumps and weaves performed together. But tricks with two dogs working together only look good when the dogs work at the same speed and with the same timing. I don't work Dax and Riker in unison because Dax moves quickly and Riker is slower and more methodical. Dax would finish a spin while Riker was only halfway through it!

> **Bet You Didn't Know**
>
> Introduce new tricks to each dog separately, allowing each the time needed to learn it well. Ask the dogs to do it together only after the new behaviors are well understood.

Multiple Owners, Dogs, and Tricks

A show made up of several dog owners and their dogs, especially of a variety of breeds, ages, sizes, and colors, can be great fun. Each dog will train and perform differently, and that adds to the excitement for your audience.

If your group has a number of different dog owners and dogs, you will need someone to take over organization of the performance. Although it might be amusing if six dogs did a spin one right after the other, it would be much more fun if each dog performed a different trick or trick routine. The organizer, or choreographer, could coordinate each dog's abilities and trick performances, assign tricks, and arrange an order of performance.

Down, Boy!

It's important that in a group such as this, all the dogs get along. If one dog is uneasy, fearful, or aggressive, the whole group could be in trouble.

Multiple Owners and Dogs of One Breed

Some one-breed clubs (such as Pug clubs or German Shepherd clubs) have put together demonstration groups that perform at breed club events, rescue organization fundraisers, and during therapy dog visits. A group of dogs, all of the same breed, with similar characteristics (both in looks and in behavior), can be very striking.

Although a group such as this might lack the variety a multiple-breed group might have, enthusiasts of the breed will be thrilled.

Drill Teams

Drill teams made up of multiple dogs and multiple owners can be awe-inspiring to watch. Years ago, when my husband and I had two German Shepherds, we formed a drill team with four other German Shepherd owners. We performed at dog shows, parades, nursing homes, and other special events and always received standing ovations.

Although teams of dogs of the same breed can be very attractive, teams can also be made up of dogs of a variety of breeds, or of mixed breeds. What's most important is the dogs have a similar working style and speed. Drill teams work in unison, so if one dog is slow, the other dogs must also work slowly.

Most drill teams perform obedience commands, including Heel, Sit, Stay, Down, Stand, and Come. During the Heel, they will make left, right, and about turns. They will walk a normal speed, walk slowly, and walk fast. Many drill teams include tricks, too, especially eye-catching ones like Weave through the legs, Heel on the right side, Follow Me, and other tricks that don't require any props and can be performed while moving.

> **Bet You Didn't Know**
> To be successful and look good to an audience, a drill team will need a caller who will direct the exercises and will critique the work and movements. The caller should be someone who has worked with the group but isn't performing with his or her own dog.

The Least You Need to Know

- 🏠 Costumes can be great fun for holidays and can add another dimension to your trick training.

- 🏠 Any costume should fit your dog well without restricting his movement; his head, legs, and tail should be able to move freely.

- 🏠 A trick routine is several tricks performed one after another and may or may not have a storyline.

- 🏠 A show consists of a trick routine, costumes, props, and a set, and a story told through the tricks and narration.

Tricks for Therapy Dogs

In This Chapter

- 🏠 Laughter is healing
- 🏠 Know your audience
- 🏠 Special tricks for therapy dogs
- 🏠 Suggestions for special events

I began training my first therapy dog in 1984. There were not many therapy dogs then, and none in my area. When I approached a local nursing home, neither they nor I had any experience with therapy dogs, but they were willing to give it a try. In 2004, we celebrated our twentieth anniversary. I had begun with a dog named Care Bear, and continued with Ursa, Dax, Kes, and am now visiting with Riker. Hopefully, the puppy, Bashir, will be able to continue the tradition.

Although trick training is not necessary for therapy dogs, and many very effective therapy dogs have never learned a single trick, tricks can make visits more appealing and the dogs more approachable.

Laughter Is Good for Us

Over twenty-five years ago, Dr. Norman Cousins said in his book *Anatomy of an Illness* that laughter helped him recover from a serious illness. Since then, many researchers have agreed that Dr. Cousins was right on target. Laughter boosts levels of endorphins, the body's natural painkillers, and suppresses levels of epinephrine, the stress hormone.

When a therapy dog walks into a nursing home or other facility, people smile. They appreciate the dog's attention and affection; they enjoy the dog owner's efforts to come and visit; and they appreciate the break in their daily routine. However, when the dog can do a few tricks (simple ones or elaborate), well, they laugh!

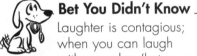

Bet You Didn't Know

Laughter is contagious; when you can laugh with your dog (but never *at* your dog), your audience will laugh, too!

Laughter is also good for the staff members of the facility you and your dog visit. Support staff, administration, and caregivers can all benefit from a visit by the dog. They appreciate the dog's affection, too, and can enjoy a few laughs when he performs some tricks.

Know Your Audience

As a therapy dog volunteer, it is vitally important to know the people you're visiting.

- 🏠 Day-care center: The children will be very young, some might or might not have been exposed to dogs, and there could be a lot of running and screaming. Simple tricks can be great amusements.

- 🏠 Kindergarten: The children will be learning to sit still, but have very short attention spans. Trick routines without storylines, or with simple, easy-to-follow storylines are fine.

🏠 Elementary school: There is a big difference in development between first grade and sixth grade; their reactions to you might vary. First graders might enjoy your visit, while sixth graders might not want to admit they still like dogs. Trick routines and shows are great here.

🏠 Hospital: People are usually injured or very ill. They are often focused inwardly, and might not want amusement. However, they might like some warmth and affection.

🏠 Skilled nursing: As with hospital patients, amusement might or might not be wanted; warmth and affection almost always is.

🏠 Retirement center and assisted living: Amusement is almost always welcomed, as is warmth and affection. Trick routines, shows, and individual tricks are welcomed at these facilities.

🏠 Hospice: Most residents welcome warmth and affection; staff members might enjoy some quiet, simple tricks.

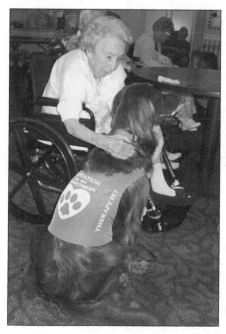

*Tricks are fun, but sometimes all that is needed is
the dog's presence, warmth, and affection.*

These are obviously general guidelines; nothing is set in concrete, and there will always be exceptions. Listen to staff members and feel free to ask questions. After all, they know their people better than you do.

Keeping It Simple at First

If you're new to therapy dog work, keep the tricks simple in the beginning. Your dog has a lot to learn about his new vocation, and adding too many tricks or difficult tricks might overwhelm him.

Some good tricks for a beginning dog could include:

- Sit Pretty: The dog could Sit Pretty when introduced to a roomful of people.

- Shake: If the dog Shakes nicely (without scratching), he could shake hands with people when introduced to them.

- Kisses: The dog should offer kisses only on command, not slather everyone with potentially unwanted slobbers.

- Bow: When leaving the room, the dog could Bow.

- Wave: When saying good-bye, the dog could Wave.

- Spin right or left: The dog could demonstrate his knowledge of left and right.

- Jump through the hoop: Ask two residents to hold a hoop and have your dog jump through it.

Down, Boy!

If you make a commitment to entertain at a facility, you must do it. If you don't show up, people will be very disappointed.

Some easy tricks, like Paws Up, work well in therapy dog work. The dog can do a Paws Up on the bedrail, side of the bed, arm of the wheelchair, or even the cross bar on a walker. Just protect the person being visited from rough paws, and brace the dog on slippery floors.

Asking people to help you and your dog makes them a part of the trick, rather than just the audience, and makes them feel needed.

Tricks can also work well when incorporated into a visit as a part of the dog's behavior. For example, one of my visits might look like this:

- 🏠 I walk into the lobby of a retirement facility where several people are waiting for us. I say, "Good morning, everyone!"

- 🏠 When they answer me with a "Good morning," I turn to my dog Riker and say to him, quietly, "Riker, Sit Pretty!" and as he does, I tell the people, "Wow! Riker's happy to see you all, too!"

- 🏠 I walk up to an individual and greet him, "Mr. Rogers, you're looking well today." I then turn to Riker, "Riker, can you shake hands with Mr. Rogers?"

- 🏠 Later, after some conversation, as I leave Mr. Rogers, I tell Riker, "Riker, can you wave to Mr. Rogers?" as I tell Mr. Rogers we'll see him again next week.

Remember, a trick routine (as described previously) and a trick show are two different things. A trick show is best performed before a crowd rather than just one person. If you're performing a show for one person, and he or she is having a bad day, or is not enthusiastic, you won't be, either. However, a group of people will band together and get each other excited. If you normally visit people in the lobby or recreation room of a facility, you can perform something slightly different each visit, or you can do something on special occasions.

You can also talk to the activities director or volunteer coordinator about special events. Many facilities regularly schedule events around holidays or they might be happy to arrange something at a time when nothing else is happening. Your trick routine or show could be a part of the holiday show, after the singers but before the main entertainment.

Troubleshooting

BARK If you would like to do something but aren't quite sure what to do, talk to the activities director. She will be thrilled that you want to help and perhaps the two of you can come up with something.

The tricks are great, the costumes are wonderful, but what's most important is that we have made a difference to the people we're visiting.

Increasing the Difficulty

If you train your dog at home (rather than at a dog training class), don't forget to add distractions to your dog's training for therapy dog work. Train with family members to add distractions; you can even ask them to heckle you a little bit. Have them clap, too, and whistle. You can also go for a walk and do some training near a school or shopping center. Just make sure you train in places other than just at home.

When you've been visiting for a while and have been doing simple tricks successfully, build on that foundation and add some difficulty. Perhaps string a few tricks together to make some routines, or teach some more elaborate tricks. The great thing about therapy visits is that most of your audience members are not going to give you a hard time if you and your dog mess up a trick or two. They appreciate your time and efforts and will root for your success.

Special Tricks for Therapy Dogs

These few tricks can make your dog a more effective therapy dog, and training these is not difficult.

Go Say Hi!

When I bring my dog close to someone on a visit, I tell him, *Go Say Hi!* rather than giving him obedience commands to put himself close to the person. If I told him to Sit and Stay, that might convey the impression that he wasn't visiting voluntarily and the person being visited might feel less than happy about petting him. Go Say Hi! is very positive and is a phrase we might use with a child.

Dog Talk _____

Go Say Hi! means "put yourself close enough to be touched and remain close while you're being petted."

You need some help to teach this command.

1. Have your volunteer sit in a chair (a wheelchair if you have one to practice with).

2. Walk your dog to the chair, and as you approach it tell him, "Fido, Go Say Hi!" and position him so he's standing sideways (parallel) to the chair with his back right under the person's hand.

3. Praise him, "Good boy to Go Say Hi!" and if he's antsy, tell him, "Stay."

4. Have your volunteer pet him for a few seconds, then praise and release him.

5. Repeat for a total of five repetitions and take a short break.

6. Come back and repeat this on both sides of the chair.

As you practice, try to phase out the Stay command, or work on giving the Stay hand signal without the verbal command. The person being visited wants to think the dog is doing this on his own; a Stay command makes it appear that the dog really doesn't want to visit.

Teaching Paws Up

In Chapter 5, you learned how to teach your dog the trick Paws Up. Go back to that section and refresh his skills so that he can put his front paws on the arm of a chair and will hold that position for fifteen to twenty seconds. When he can do that, he's ready to continue training.

1. Borrow a wheelchair, if you can, from the facility you visit regularly.

2. Put the brakes on the chair so it won't move.

3. With treats in your pocket and a leash on your dog, approach the chair from the side.

4. Pat the arm of the chair and tell your dog, "Fido, Paws Up."

5. When he puts his paws on the arm of the chair, praise him and pop a treat in his mouth.

6. Release him, praise him again, and move him away from the chair.

7. Repeat for a total of five repetitions and take a break.

Repeat this for several training sessions, working on both sides of the wheelchair. Gradually ask your dog to hold the Paws Up position for slightly longer, up to thirty seconds each time. If he is healthy, strong, and has a good back and no hip disease, ask him to hold it for up to a minute.

When your dog is holding the position well, begin petting him as he's doing the Paws Up. After all, he will be doing this so that someone can reach him, so get him used to being petted while his paws are on the arm of the wheelchair. Pet his face, rub his head, and scratch behind his ears.

Down, Boy!
Dogs with physical disabilities in their back, rear legs, or hips should not do the Paws Up.

If your dog will be doing a Paws Up on a slippery floor, you can brace him by placing one of your legs behind his hips, with your foot behind his rear paws so they don't slide. When you first do this, your dog might be startled and jump, so practice it at home. The first time you do it, let him turn around and see what you're doing, then ask him to do a Paws Up again.

BARK

Troubleshooting
If your dog is antsy and wants to keep moving while doing a Paws Up, tell him to Stay. He knows what this means and it should calm him.

If your dog is tall enough, he can also learn to do a Paws Up on the crossbar of a walker. However, when you ask him to do this, get a good grip on the walker first. Walkers are not very substantial, and you don't want it, your dog, and the person using the walker to collapse in a heap on the floor!

Getting Up on the Bed

Most dogs are more than willing to get up on the bed, any bed, but therapy dogs must learn how to get up on a bed gently, without hurting the resident, and then lie still.

1. You can teach this at home first. Ask your volunteer to get comfortable in your bed, with a blanket over him.

2. Walk your dog to the foot of your bed, facing toward the head of the bed.

3. Tell your dog, "Fido, On the Bed," and encourage him to hop up.

4. Keeping a hand on your dog's collar, walk him next to the person on the bed until he reaches their knees.

5. Tell him, "Fido, Down." Praise him when he lies down.

Down, Boy!

Not all facilities want dogs on the bed, and not all people want the dog to get up there, so always ask permission first, both from the facility and from the individual in the bed.

6. Then tell him, "Fido, Crawl" and have him crawl forward a few inches at a time until he reaches the person's hand.

7. Praise him and tell him to Stay.

When your dog is on the bed, make sure he remains still. He should never step on the person, lie down next to their face, or roll around or thrash. If your dog gets too excited, have him jump off the bed.

Special Events

Unfortunately, living in a facility is never like living at home, and sometimes residents complain that life is just too institutionalized. You can't change that, but you can help the activities director add a little spice to the institutional life.

Easter Egg Hunt

Easter should be celebrated as a nondenominational holiday so as not to offend people of different beliefs. An Easter egg hunt is as nondenominational as a game could get.

The game is best done with a group of visiting therapy dogs. Have the dog owners get together and stuff several dozen plastic Easter eggs with dog treats. They can be carried into the facility in an Easter basket. While the dogs wait outside, the activities director can have staff members assist the residents in hiding the eggs in the lobby or recreation room. When all the eggs are hidden, the dogs can come in (on leash, of course) and find the eggs. The dog who finds the most eggs is presented with a special treat.

This is a great event because the residents soon begin to cheer for the dogs, "There's one!" "Don't forget the one under the green chair!" At one Easter egg hunt, a frail, elderly lady took my dog's leash from me, saying, "You're moving too slow! He's not getting enough eggs!"

 **Down, Boy!**

Always make sure all of the plastic eggs are found and accounted for; you don't want someone to step on or sit on one of them later.

The group could also have some treats for the residents after the egg hunt is over. Some Easter chocolate (or sugar-free treats) is great, and perhaps some tea or coffee. A visit afterward gives everyone a chance to talk about it, laugh, and congratulate the winning dog.

Fourth of July Drill Team

If you have several dogs who are very good at their obedience training and owners who know their right from their left, a doggy drill
team is quite impressive. If dogs and owners are in red, white, and
blue, it can be very patriotic, especially if you have some patriotic
music, too.

A drill routine doesn't have to be elaborate. All the dogs should
be on leash, and all the dogs and owners should work in unison,
keeping an eye on each other to keep together. Someone else can
call the commands that have been previously practiced. (Someone
who is not handling a dog needs to be the caller—but someone who
works with the group, not someone from "outside.")

If you have a large group, you can do this outside where all the
residents can see, such as a parking lot. Or if you just have three or
four dogs and handlers, try it in the recreation room or lobby.

Before your show, hand each resident a small American flag to
get them in the mood. Afterward, talk to those residents who might
be veterans and invite them to share some of their experiences. You
would be amazed at the heroes who might be in your audience.

Halloween

Halloween is made for therapy dogs! If you visit with a group of
dogs, have all the dogs and owners come in costume. You can have
the residents vote on their favorites, with the activities director tally-
ing the votes. Categories could include scariest costume, best dog
and owner costume, most original, most patriotic, and silliest. Add
your own categories.

You should bring some dog treats to be handed out as prizes and
perhaps some cookies and brownies to be shared with the residents
after the judging is complete.

One year, we had seventy dogs at our Halloween party and over one hundred people. It was huge! People had a great time and talked about it for months afterward. People laughed, talked, shared memories, and petted dogs. Other than the mess we had to clean up afterward (it was a big party!), there was no downside to it.

The more approachable a therapy dog is, either doing tricks or in costume (or both!), the more effective he will be.

Christmas

Christmas, like Easter, should be celebrated as a nondenominational holiday so as not to offend people of varying beliefs.

Many therapy dog groups use Christmas as an excuse to dress up their dogs. There will be dogs in Santa suits or reindeer antlers, and dog owners dressed as elves, Mrs. Santa, or Santa himself. Candy canes can be handed out to those who can have sugar, and holiday cards can be given to all.

Our therapy dog group each year recruits local elementary school teachers to have their classes make hand-made cards. We gather the cards, and then hand them out to the people we visit during the holidays.

If anyone in your group still has an instant camera (one that prints photos immediately), those photos make treasured gifts. Take a picture of a resident with a dog dressed in his holiday finery and you'll find that photo prominently displayed forever.

Local Community Events

If your local community has some special events, coordinate a visit to go along with it. Many of the people you visit might not be able to see the local squash parade or go to the garlic festival, so bring the party to them. It's not hard to make a themed visit; some special tricks, a few decorations, and some advance coordination with the activities director are all it takes.

The Least You Need to Know

- Laughter is good for all of us and is best shared. Laugh with your dog and laugh with the people you'll be visiting.

- Know your audience so you know what kind of tricks and trick routines to train.

- Keep your tricks simple in the beginning, but with experience and practice, feel free to get more elaborate.

- Every holiday can be an excuse for a therapy dog party!

Chapter 15

Dancing with Your Dog

In This Chapter

- 🏠 Dancing with your dog for fun
- 🏠 Finding the music
- 🏠 Building a routine
- 🏠 Having fun with your dog

People who love music also love to move with the music. You feel the rhythm, the words touch you, and the melody affects your soul. Pretty soon the toes begin tapping, the fingers twitch, the body sways, and suddenly you're dancing!

Did you ever think about dancing with your dog? Well, you can, and no, it's not weird! Freestyle is a new dog sport that encourages dog owners to dance with their dogs. Dog owners can do this for fun, at home, at demonstrations, or on therapy dog visits. They can also dance competitively for titles.

Discovering Freestyle

Freestyle is a new sport that emphasizes the teamwork between dog and owner as they dance a self-choreographed routine to music.

The choreography doesn't have to be elaborate, but it does need to be original and unique. The routines highlight the strengths of each individual dog-and-owner team.

The steps and movements of a freestyle dance combine human dance steps and sports with canine obedience exercises and trick training and can even pull elements from equine dressage to create a totally unique activity. Several organizations sponsor competitions and award titles, and each of these provides guidelines for competition (see "Competitive Freestyle," later in this chapter) but otherwise, the moves used depend upon the dog and owner.

In competitions, the teams are usually dressed up (either in finery or costumes) and the outfits complement the music and routine. A team dancing to a Latin beat and music might wear costumes with a Latin flavor, for example. The dogs' costumes often consist of a decorated collar, decorated bands on the dog's wrists and ankles, and perhaps a vest. Rarely is the canine costume a full-bodied costume such as worn for Halloween.

Down, Boy!

The dog's costume should allow for freedom of movement.

Freestyle is one of those activities where you can compete and win titles, or you can enjoy the sport on your own terms. If you enjoy doing things with your dog and you love music, you can make this into an enjoyable activity for both of you.

Getting Started

Canine freestyle came into being in the 1990s. Several different people have taken credit for it, but no matter who first danced with his or her dog, this is a new sport with more and more people discovering it each year. Freestyle is a sport whose time has come.

The first thing you need to do is decide what you would like this dance routine to convey to your audience. Do you want to show off your dog's natural athleticism? His beauty? The teamwork the two of you share? Or the joy you take in music? Think about what you want your dance to show and keep that in mind as you choose your music and begin choreographing the steps of your dance.

Choosing Your Music

Before you put together a routine, you need to choose some music. You will want something with a strong beat that will help you and your dog move. A subtle beat is not good here; the beat must permeate your soul. The music can be instrumental or have vocals; that's your decision.

The rhythms of the music should suit your dog. If you have a quick, active, light-footed dog and use slower music with a heavy beat, your dog might not be able to find that beat. Or he might not be happy to move with it. On the other hand, a heavy-bodied, steady dog should not be asked to keep up with quick, light music. The music you choose, no matter what type, should have a rhythm that suits your dog's natural way of moving.

Sometimes the easiest way to choose your music is to grab your CDs and begin playing them. Clear the living room floor of all obstacles and begin moving to the music. Invite your dog to join you and see which music he reacts to most positively. Play some rock, country, jazz, and blues. Put on some classical music, too. Don't forget to listen to some show tunes. When you can narrow the list to four or five songs that you and your dog both like, set them aside. Play them again the next day and see which song really stands out.

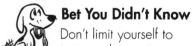 **Bet You Didn't Know**
Don't limit yourself to just popular music. Instead, listen to a wide variety of different types and styles of music; you might find something totally different that is perfect for you and your dog.

Do think about the style or ethnicity of the music as you make your decision, because that could have some bearing on your costume should you decide to do demonstrations or competitions. If you choose a Scottish ballad, for example, you won't be wearing a Latin costume. Your choice of music will have to match your likes (and dislikes) for attire.

Bet You Didn't Know
Choose a piece of music that you won't mind hearing over and over again.

Beginning to Move

Put your music in the CD player, clear out the living room floor (or go out in the backyard), invite your dog to join you, and move to the music. What movements feel natural? You can use dance steps and moves that you've used before, perhaps from country line dancing, or square dancing, even ballroom dancing or a few polka steps. Let the beat of the music find you and just move.

As you move, encourage your dog to follow you, by moving your body, stretching out and moving your arms, smiling at your dog, and giving him verbal praise. When you do this, note what he is doing. Is he finding the beat of the music with his steps? Is his tail wagging? Praise him as he follows you, or as you follow him.

BARK Troubleshooting
If your dog hesitates to move to the music, ask him to do a trick or two that he really enjoys, then praise him. When he's doing something, get him excited and keep him moving.

The goal in the beginning is to find some natural movements that suit the music you've chosen. After you both have loosened up and can move to the music, you can begin building a dance routine.

Some people hesitate to become involved in freestyle because they can't dance. "I have two left feet!" one friend said. Although freestyle is all about dancing, at the same time dancing isn't required.

You can dance, but you don't have to. I know, that's a contradiction; so let me explain.

Freestyle requires both the dog and handler to move to the music. If that's dancing to you, super! However, specific dance steps that might be required for line dancing, ballet, or the tango are not required. So people who tend to step on a human partner's toes and who cannot tell their left from their right can participate in freestyle with no worries.

Moving to the Beat

There is a variety of movements you can include in your dance routine. Some come from obedience exercises, some from trick training, a few from human dance steps, and some even from equine dressage.

- 🏠 Obedience Heel: Dancing is all about moving together, and there is nothing like obedience heelwork to keep a team working together.

- 🏠 Trick Training Heel: In Chapter 7, you learned the trick Other Side, where your dog learned to Heel on the right side, too.

- 🏠 Back and Follow Me: Also taught in Chapter 7, the Back and Follow Me can easily be incorporated into a dance routine.

- 🏠 Changes of Pace: Slow steps, fast steps, and steps to the right or left can easily be worked into any routine.

- 🏠 Turns, Spins, and Circles: Dancing is all about moving, so incorporate movements and patterns that suit you, your dog, and the music.

- 🏠 Weaves: The Weave (also taught in Chapter 7) can easily be incorporated into a dance.

Bet You Didn't Know

Teach your dog to walk slow or fast with you by simply changing your speed of walking and encouraging your dog (with your voice and training treats) to maintain his position with you.

🏠 Tricks: Bow, Sit Pretty, Shake, Wave, and many other tricks (many of these were taught in Chapter 5) can easily be incorporated into dance routines.

🏠 Jumps: Your dog can jump your leg or through your arms, as was taught in Chapter 6.

Heeling on the left side (an obedience exercise) and on the right side (a trick) can both be a part of a freestyle routine.

As you put together a routine, think about the space you will want to cover for your dance, or the space restrictions you might face. If you will be dancing in the recreation room of a nursing home for a therapy dog visit, you might not have much room. However, if you will eventually be competing in freestyle, you could have a forty-foot-by-fifty-foot ring in which to move. In either case, you want to cover the space equally instead of focusing on one particular area. Your audience, all of your audience, deserves to see both you and your dog as you dance.

There is normally a front or focal point in every space. In a nursing home, this could be where most of your audience is gathered. In a competition, this would be where the judges are seated. Your dance could begin and end facing this point. However, the rest of your dance should give your entire audience equal viewing time.

As you begin, mark off a space like this and just move around it with your dog. Do some heel-work, a few spins, and a little weave. Go back and forth and find out what it feels like to move through this space. How big or how small is this area? This will help you as you begin to add steps and build your routine.

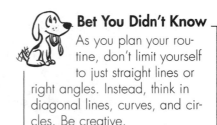

Bet You Didn't Know

As you plan your routine, don't limit yourself to just straight lines or right angles. Instead, think in diagonal lines, curves, and circles. Be creative.

When you first begin, your dog isn't going to understand what you want, so make this fun and use lots of encouragement.

Your various moves should flow with and suit the beat or rhythm of the music. The moves should flow easily from one to the next. For example, here are some potential movements for a simple first routine:

- The music begins with your dog standing by your side, looking at you.

- You both walk forward together a couple of steps.

- Your dog then moves to your right side and you continue forward another two steps.

- You then back up and your dog follows you.

- You stop and your dog circles you.

Throughout this, you are both swaying to the music, and you are moving your arms to the music and your dog's tail is wagging.

- You circle to the right as your dog weaves through your legs.

- You turn around and your dog follows you.

- You circle to the left as your dog weaves back the other direction.

Visualize each movement following the one before it, flowing nicely with the music. After all, you're dancing!

When you feel more comfortable, add some other moves. You can perform some dance steps from dances you know, such as line dancing, square dancing, or even ballet. Encourage your dog to follow you and give him some commands, such as Bow, Weave, or Wave.

You can also teach him some entirely new things just for your dancing. If there is a local horse show, go watch the dressage; it's absolutely amazing. You can borrow some movements from dressage for your dog. Use the training skills you've learned in this book: break the behavior into small behavior steps, reinforce each step, and don't move on to the next one until the first is learned.

Competitive Freestyle

Freestyle began as another way to have fun, and demonstrations were given at dog events in the early 1990s. The first organization to hold competitions was Musical Canine Sports International (MCSI). Costumes and a variety of styles of dancing soon followed, and the sport continued to gain popularity. Today, several organizations sponsor events and award titles. Appendix B lists a number of organizations (and their websites) and resources for the sport.

World Canine Freestyle Organization (WCFO)

The World Canine Freestyle Organization (WCFO) offers two styles of competition: Heelwork to Music and Musical Freestyle. Heelwork to Music is, as the name implies, based on heelwork. There is no jumping or weaves, and the dog works very close to the owner. The dog and owner competing in Musical Freestyle can be much more innovative as just about anything goes as long as it's safe for both dog and owner.

There are several levels of competition, including beginners, novice, intermediate, and advanced, both for Heelwork to Music and Musical Freestyle. WCFO welcomes both purebred dogs and mixed breeds of any size. Puppies may not title until over six months of age.

Canine Freestyle Federation (CFF)

The Canine Freestyle Federation (CFF) is an international organization dedicated to the sport of freestyle. CFF encourages both purebreds and mixed breeds. Dogs under six months of age cannot compete. The CFF encourages originality and creativity, and urges competitors to remember spectator appeal when designing their routines.

CFF offers titles in a number of different levels of competition, from Level I through IV, and for individual dogs and multiple dogs. In Level I, required elements that must be included in the routine include heel work, front work (dog in front), pace changes, turns and pivots, circles, and spirals or serpentines. The difficulty increases through the levels, with the required elements for Level IV including right and left side heelwork, front work, changes of pace, turns and pivots, circles or serpentines, backing, lateral work right and left, and distance work (dog at a distance from owner).

Musical Dog Sport Association (MDSA)

The Musical Dog Sport Association states that "Training, dedication, teamwork, music, and creativity all combine to create a unique performance equally supported by both members but highlighting the canine partner."

MDSA is a new organization that is still evolving and offers two programs: Heelwork to Music and Rhythmic Freestyle. Heelwork to Music emphasizes the dog and owner working together in unity, close in proximity, and with movements that flow together. Rhythmic Freestyle is more creative, with movements from other sources, such as those found in equine dressage and canine trick training.

When you combine obedience skills, trick training, dance, and music, you can't help but have fun!

Working with Other Groups

There are several other groups centered around freestyle. Some present demonstrations, others offer training, and a few sponsor competitions. You can find out more about these groups by checking out their websites (see Appendix B for website addresses). If there is a group in your area, go watch one of their events—it's fascinating.

Freestyle for Fun

Freestyle is a competitive sport, but there is no requirement that you must compete. This is a fun activity for therapy dogs, dogs doing demonstrations at schools or during other canine events, or simply having fun with your dog. A friend of mine (the one with two left feet!) said she could never dance in public, even with her dog, but she enjoys dancing at home and is thrilled to find another way to spend time with her dog.

The Least You Need to Know

- Freestyle is a new sport that combines dancing, canine obedience, and trick skills, as well as elements from equine dressage, with music.

- Your music can be any style or type, with vocals or instrumental, but should have a good beat.

- When initially building your routine, just listen to the music with your dog and move.

- Freestyle can be competitive, with several organizations sponsoring competitions and titles, or can be for fun and entertainment.

Chapter 16

Creating a Star!

In This Chapter

- 🏠 Any dog can be a star
- 🏠 Some tricks of the trade
- 🏠 Writing your dog's resumé
- 🏠 It's a tough business

Dogs are popular today in print ads as well as on television and in movies. Flip through the newspaper or a magazine and you can find dogs in ads for carpets, room deodorizers, SUVs, pickup trucks, and much more. On television or in the movies, dogs have starring roles, such as Eddie on *Frasier*, or have supporting roles as a part of the family.

Much of this popularity is due to the numbers of dogs kept as pets, but it also stems from a change in how we think about our dogs. Whereas a generation ago, dogs were thought of as pets or possessions, today they are more often considered members of the family. Because dogs today are cared for as family members, their importance in our lives has increased dramatically. The media reflects that change in status.

Can Your Dog Be a Star?

My dog, Dax, has appeared in a movie. She wasn't the star, but she didn't end up on the cutting room floor, either. She did a great job, got compliments from the director, and was much more professional than many of the human actors.

Dax appeared in this movie because a friend of ours knew she was well trained and liked to retrieve. Our friend (who is also a dog trainer) had been contacted by a casting agent. The director of the movie needed a dog who would retrieve a baseball during a baseball game, and who could also participate in several other scenes in the movie. The casting agent also wanted a dog who looked "like the dog next door." Dax, a black tri-colored Australian Shepherd, does not look exotic and weighs about forty pounds, so can definitely pass for the dog next door!

I was faxed a copy of the scenes that Dax would be in, including the directions for her movements (what she would need to do) and the dates, times, and addresses where she had to report. The next two weeks were spent training Dax for her scenes. She already knew everything that was going to be asked of her (Sit, Down, Stay, Heel, Retrieve, and Come) but she would be doing all of these things at a distance from me, so I wanted to work on hand signals from about twenty feet away.

 Bet You Didn't Know

I was able to train and work Dax myself because I am a known dog trainer. Some dogs in movies are trained and worked by professional dog trainers even when those dogs are privately owned.

The movie was about a young man who enlisted in the military and went to war. Dax played his dog at home prior to enlisting, so she was only in the first few scenes. The movie opened with a dirt lot baseball game. Dax was sitting by the sidelines with the young man's girlfriend. The game was tied, the young man's team was in the field, and the opposing team had people on base. It looked like the hero's team was going to lose when the opposing team hit the ball that would bring in the winning run. The infielders missed the ball and it headed to right field. Dax bolted from the girlfriend and grabbed the ball. Running as hard as she could, Dax carried the ball to home plate where she tagged out the runner who was trying to win the game. It was a great scene!

In other scenes, Dax was not the center of attention, but instead, simply played the male star's pet dog. She followed him around, sat next to him, and comforted his girlfriend when he enlisted in the military and left home.

Any number of dogs could have done what Dax did, and that's the way this business works. To break into the business, you will have to promote your dog so people know who he is, what he looks like, and what his skills are. You'll want to decide whether you want to work with an agent. And then you will train your dog, train him again, and train him some more! But most of all, you will have to work hard and you'll need lots of good luck.

Enzo has starred in a number of print ads for a major pet supply store.

Looking Good!

When a dog is needed for a part, either in a commercial, a television show, or a movie, the people in charge of casting might have some specific directions as to what kind of dog is needed. For example, for Dax's part in the movie, they wanted a medium-sized "dog next door." They didn't want a dog that looked exotic, or expensive, or too different. But that was just this movie; other times the book upon which the movie was based might have stated the breed of dog, and the casting people will try to match that. Businesses contracting the making of a commercial might have instructions as to the breed or mixture of breeds. No breed or mixture of breeds is out of the question. It simply depends upon the needs and wants of those in charge.

Other times, the director might say, "I'll know the right dog when I see him." In those situations, dogs of every size, shape, color, and breed (or mixtures thereof) may apply.

All dogs applying for a part or position should be well groomed. That means clean, free of parasites of any kind, and brushed and combed. Fancy haircuts are usually not recommended unless specifically requested. Hair dressings, hair pieces, and costumes are not usually recommended, either, unless requested.

Down, Boy!

Dogs facing a health challenge, including skin or coat disorders, should not apply until they are healthy again.

Behaving Well

The cutest dog in the world will not get a job unless he's well behaved. Time is money, and no one will be willing to give your dog excess time to perform. Training needs to be done ahead of time, especially basic obedience training, as well as the training needed for the performance.

Dax was very well trained prior to her movie part; however, when we got the directions for her part, I spent two weeks working with her so she knew exactly what she needed to do for each command. As a result, she needed only one or two takes for her shots. The big baseball game shot she did on her first try. Although the director did a few more shots for the human actors (and she repeated her performance each time), he was thrilled with what she did and how she did it.

The basic obedience commands are a necessity for all performers, not just for their work in front of the camera but also for good behavior behind the scenes. Tricks are always good, too, and might give you an edge in getting a part. Just make sure you can direct your dog from a distance so you can be off camera when he performs.

Your dog must also be well socialized to a variety of people of all sizes, ethnicities, shapes, and ages. You can't risk having your dog react poorly because there's a small child on the set or a person of a different heritage.

Make sure, too, that prior to applying for a job, your dog is used to different places. Take him to the hardware store and pet store, walk him around the boats at the harbor, and let him hear motorcycles, garbage trucks, and vacuum cleaners. Make sure he won't jump when bright lights flash.

Bet You Didn't Know

Don't let your dog get in the habit of looking or sniffing at cameras. Rarely is the dog asked to look directly at a camera, so this can be bad habit. Instead, work on the Watch Me and have him look at you even when someone else has a camera pointed at him.

Tricks Your Dog Can Use

Many of the tricks taught in this book can be used in print ads, commercials, television, and movies. The most important are tricks that can be incorporated into a storyline and those that show emotion. Bow, Say Your Prayers, Belly Up, Spin, Crawl, and Retrieve are all good ones.

What's important is to develop some tricks that your dog will do reliably, every time you ask, no matter what the distractions are. When those tricks are very reliable, you can then add them to your dog's resumé.

Your dog should be proficient in all the basic obedience commands and quite a few tricks.

 Bet You Didn't Know _____

Reliable performances are important. Your dog must perform his commands (obedience and trick) when asked. You cannot beg him to perform by repeating a command five or six times. He must do things as you ask him to do them.

Hitting the Target

One of the most important skills any actor needs is the ability to hit a target. All of filming is about being where you're supposed to be when the camera is rolling. Human actors must hit their targets, and they get in trouble when they don't; if your dog knows how to hit a target, directors will love you for training him. Here's how to teach him.

1. Choose something that can be a moveable target. You're going to use this throughout your dog's career, so make it something you can easily replace. A small paper plate, a little paper target, or even a brightly colored piece of paper will work.

2. Hold the target in your hand and ask your dog to Shake.

3. When he lifts his paw to your hand, tell him, "Fido, good to Shake! Good *Target!*" and pop a treat in his mouth.

4. Repeat for a total of five repetitions and take a break.

5. When you train the second set of five repetitions, use the command "Fido, Target, Shake!" and praise him.

6. During the third set of repetitions, emphasize the word *target* more, "Fido, TARGET, Shake," praise him, and give him a treat.

Dog Talk

Target is your dog's command to go to his spot.

When he will touch the target in your hand upon hearing the word, you're ready to move on. From now on, stop saying *shake* and use only *target*.

7. Now rest your hand on the floor, with the target still in your hand (target up, of course) and ask your dog to touch it, "Fido, Target!"

8. Praise him when he does.

9. Repeat for a total of five repetitions and take a break.

Troubleshooting

If your dog hesitates to touch your hand on the floor, add a couple more training steps. Have him touch your hand part way down toward the floor, halfway to the floor, and then finally on the floor.

When your dog is touching the target on your hand with your hand resting on the floor, you're ready to continue.

10. Place the target on the floor about a foot away from your dog. Tell him, "Fido, Target!"

11. When he touches it with one paw, praise him and pop a treat in his mouth. Make sure his paw is still on the target when you give him the treat.

12. Repeat for a total of five repetitions and take a break.

Over several training sessions throughout the next few days, send your dog to his target from different places: left, right, front, and back. Make sure he always touches it with one paw. Do this five times and take a break.

When he can go to the target from any direction, begin increasing the distance he needs to walk to go to the target. Begin just a couple of feet away and increase it gradually until he can hit the target from twenty to thirty feet away.

Then when he hits it, praise him and tell him, "Fido, Stay!" and go to him to praise him. You don't want him to hit the target and then dash away for the treat. He is to hit the target and stay until he receives a release or another command.

Getting a Paw in the Door

If you would like your dog to hit the big time (or the big screen), he will need a resumé just like the major human stars have. That means he will need to do some work locally.

Each of these has potential to use a dog:

🏠 Community theatre: Almost every city has a community theatre group. Sometimes it's through the high school, community or junior college, or the university, or it might be an amateur, semi-professional, or even a professional drama club.

- Competitions: Competitions are held through dog breed clubs, training groups, and rescue organizations. They might also be held as fundraisers for animal shelters.

- Newspapers and magazines: Dogs can appear both in advertising and in photographs to illustrate an article.

- Businesses: Many businesses design their own advertisements.

Approaching businesses can be difficult; it's hard to be taken seriously when you walk up and say, "Hey, do you want to use my dog in your advertising program?" You need to present as professional an appearance as possible. That means approaching the businesses professionally, with a letter, your dog's resumé and photo, and a follow-up phone call. Or you can hire an agent to do the footwork for you.

Bet You Didn't Know
Don't assume only pet-related businesses use dogs in advertisements. A dog makes people look warm and caring, so many businesses in a variety of fields use dogs in their ads.

Agent or No Agent?

Agents work for a percentage of the income you (or your dog) bring in, with most agents collecting between ten and twenty percent. If you're just bringing in minimum wage, this isn't much money. However, if you're collecting hundreds of dollars per shoot, that percentage is higher, too.

Some dog owners don't like to share the income, and that's your right; you can do all the work and keep all the income (after Uncle Sam collects his, that is!). But before you decide that an agent isn't right for you, make sure you have the time to do what the agent normally does.

- 🏠 The agent knows people and touches base with them regularly. "Hey, Joe, how's it going? What have you got on tap? What do you need?" The agent can then go through his list of clients and set up appointments for those who might fit those needs.

- 🏠 The agent can keep your dog's name and photo in front of people, mailing them out or handing them out at business meetings and lunches.

- 🏠 The agent hears about casting calls and can get you to them.

- 🏠 The agent follows up after casting calls or appointments and tries to get you a deal.

- 🏠 The agent knows how to bargain for more money and knows how far to push. He knows what the market is paying.

- 🏠 The agent will read through your contract first, see any problems, and discuss them with you. He can also ask for any changes you might want.

- 🏠 The agent will get you your check. (Checks are always slow!)

If you have the time and knowledge to do this yourself, great! You might be able to save some money. But if you don't have any contacts in this business, you might want to hire an agent.

The best referral for an agent is word of mouth. If you know someone whose dog, cat, bird, or horse is represented by an agent, find out who the agent is. Ask how happy they are with the agent, how much work the agent does for them, and how quickly the checks arrive.

If you don't know anyone who has had their pet involved in this business, you can do an Internet search for an animal agent (see Appendix B). However, be careful: There are scam artists in this business as in any other. If you must pay cash up front for the agent, ask why. In addition, if the promises sound too good to be true, they probably are. No responsible agent will promise to make your dog a star; it just isn't that easy.

An agent will want some information about your dog, including:

- Name
- Age or date of birth
- Male or female, spayed or neutered
- Vaccination dates
- Health
- Breed, or mixture of breeds
- Color and markings
- Weight
- Coat type and look

You will be required to provide normal information, including the city and state where you live, a cell phone and home phone number, and whether or not you can be readily available for emergency or last-minute calls.

Questions about your dog's training will also be asked. For example, can your dog do the following?

- Hit a mark
- Lic down
- Down Stay
- Sit
- Sit Stay
- Lie on his side
- Paws Up
- Shake
- Sit up or Sit Pretty
- Speak

You will also be asked about your dog's socialization to people and his environment. The agent will want to know if your dog can handle strange things. For example …

- Does your dog react to large, noisy, moving objects?
- Does your dog react to different dogs?
- Is he okay with other animals?
- Can he work in close proximity to other animals?
- Does he travel well?
- Is he cage or crate trained?
- Is he motivated by food?
- Does he like to swim?
- Does he like people he doesn't know?
- Is he okay with children and babies?
- Is he okay with elderly people?

Although many casting directors want generic dogs, it never hurts to be cute and different!

All of these questions will help the agent decide whether to accept your dog as a client. If he does, he needs to know these things to find work that will suit both your dog and the people who need to hire a dog.

Photos, Please!

Just like human actors, your dog will need some photos. These should be of professional quality. Snapshots, out-of-focus shots, and cluttered-looking photos will not work. Although professional photographs cost money, if you really want to do this with your dog, you need to make the investment.

Find a photographer who has experience taking photos of pets and ask to see his work. The photos should be crisp and clear, no fuzzy edges, and no fancy effects. The background should be uncluttered. If you don't know of a photographer, ask the agent you've been talking to for a referral.

Most agents want two photos, a head shot and a body shot. The head shot should show expression; your dog should look alive and not like a cardboard cutout. The full body shot should show your dog's physique (build and body proportions). If your dog does some different tricks, take a couple of those, too. However, you don't want more than four photos; potential employers will not look at more than that.

> **Bet You Didn't Know**
> When you choose the photos to use, evaluate them as a potential employer rather than as the owner of a really well-loved dog!

Writing a Resumé

Your dog's resumé will accompany his photos when the agent (or you) tries to get him some work. The resumé should be brief and to the point, and yet convey the abilities and personality of your dog.

Here is Dax's resumé:

Name: Dax

Gender: Female, spayed

Date of Birth: June 15th, 1994

Breed: Australian Shepherd

Coat color: Black, with white and copper markings

Coat type: Medium length, shiny and wavy

Eye color: Brown

Height: 18 inches at the shoulder

Weight: 45 pounds

Dax resides in Oceanside, CA. She is within driving range of any Southern California studio or location, but is willing to travel if travel expenses are paid. She is crate trained and travels well.

Dax has appeared in one movie and one movie trailer. She received rave reviews from movie goers. The directors for her work, Mr. John Doe and Ms. Sally Smith, both enjoyed her work and work ethic. They may be contacted for referrals.

Dax has also appeared in several magazines, including *Dog Fancy*, *Dog World*, *AKC Gazette*, and others.

Dax is very well trained, works from verbal commands and hand signals, and knows a variety of tricks. She is a fast learner and can pick up new commands and tricks in a very short period of time. She has a confident personality and is unfazed by sights, sounds, and smells in her environment. She is a certified therapy dog, has earned several obedience titles, is an avid agility dog, and is herding-instinct tested.

If your dog doesn't have any movie experience, think of other activities he has done that you can put on his resumé. Is he a therapy dog? Has he participated in a trick-training contest? You need something to show the person doing the hiring that your dog has potential.

When Your Dog Is Hired

When your dog is offered a job, read the contract carefully. Read all the small print and make sure you understand it and are willing to comply with it all. You might want to hire an attorney to explain the fine print to you. If you have an agent, he or she will.

You might be asked to supply insurance to cover your dog and his actions before, during, and after the shoots. This isn't unusual, so don't be surprised if you're asked to do this.

If your dog will be working with another trainer, arrange to meet her. Introduce yourself and your dog, and find out how the process works. She might have you leave your dog with her for training. Or, if your dog is already proficient, she might ask to keep him for a few days to bond with and get to know him.

If you are going to be training and working your dog, find out exactly what you need to do, when, where, and how. Know the details and write them down; don't rely on your memory. You don't want to be a no-show for shooting!

Troubleshooting

If you have trouble with the training, or if your dog has not mastered the needed skills, call your point of contact prior to the shoot. You don't want to show up unprepared!

When you go to a shoot, bring your dog's crate, water and a water bowl, training treats, a couple of special toys, a brush and comb, and a leash. Find out where you can set up (He will not have a dressing room!) and where he can go to relieve himself.

Be prepared to protect your dog; this is a tough business. The business is overseen by many rules, regulations, and laws, but you are your dog's protector. Don't let him be overworked, and make sure he has time to relax, play, go potty, eat, and drink.

The Least You Need to Know

- With lots of hard work and quite a bit of good luck, any well-behaved, socialized, and superbly trained dog can be a star!

- Obedience and trick training can make your dog a more valuable commodity.

- An agent is paid from the money your dog earns, but can take over a lot of the work of promoting your dog and finding new jobs.

- This is a tough business; make sure you protect your dog at all times.

Appendix A

A Doggy Dictionary

adolescence   The stage of development in which the puppy is becoming an adult and is striving for independence.

aggression   A hostile reaction to stimuli. This is the fight part of the fight-or-flight instinct.

agility   An obstacle course for dogs that can be for fun or for competition.

alternative behavior   A behavior or action that takes the place of an unwanted behavior or action.

Back   Command that means walk backward from me in a straight line.

basic obedience commands   These traditionally include Sit, Down, Stay, Heel, and Come, but can also include Release and Watch Me.

behavior modification   The process of changing behavior. It combines training with an understanding of why dogs do things, and involves changing the dog, the owner, and the environment.

bond, bonding   The relationship between a dog and his owner that results in a strong emotional connection.

Bow   Command that means lower your front end to the ground, keeping your hips elevated, and wait for a release to end the trick.

buckle collar   A nylon or leather collar that fastens with some kind of a buckle. Not a slip collar.

carting   A sport and occupation where the dog pulls a wagon or sulky and either a load or a passenger.

Come   Command that means run directly to the caller, ignoring all distractions.

conformation competition   Dog shows for evaluating a dog as compared to others of his breed and in accordance with the breed standard.

Crawl   Command that means lie down and pull yourself forward without getting up.

Dance   Command that means stand upright on your rear legs and move around; dance.

distractions   Things that can break the dog's concentration.

Down   Command that means lie down on the floor or the ground and hold still.

exercise   Physical activity or movement.

Find It   Command that means search for the named or indicated item.

Follow Me   Command that means walk directly behind me, following in my footsteps.

freestyle   An activity where dog and owner both dance to music.

Give It   Command that means release the item into my hand without playing tug of war.

goals, long range   Objectives you are working toward that will take time and effort to accomplish.

goals, short range Training steps; a daily goal might be one, two, or even three training steps.

Go To Sleep Command that means lie down on your side, with your head down, and hold still.

head halter A training tool much like a halter on a horse.

Heel Command that means walk by my left side, with your shoulder next to my leg.

housetraining The process of teaching the dog to relieve himself in a specific area, to relieve himself on command, and to stop himself from going in the house.

instinct Inborn urges to respond to things in a specific manner.

interruption A verbal sound that stops unwanted behavior as it is happening.

Jump (or Hup!) Command that means jump over the obstacle indicated.

leader To your dog, his leader is much like a parent. The leader guides the dog and sets limits.

Leave It Command that means ignore the distraction.

Let's Go Command that means follow me on the leash, keeping it slack, with no pulling.

lure A lure leads the dog from one position into another, or from one place to another.

motivator Something your dog likes (treats or toys) to gain his cooperation in training.

muzzle The part of the skull from under the eyes forward to the nose, top and lower jaws, and the supporting bone.

negative attention Something negative (scolding, correction) sought by the dog solely (by misbehaving) to get the owner's attention.

off-leash work   Means the dog is working for you (as compared to ignoring you) without a leash connected to his collar.

Other Paw   Command that means lift your left paw toward my hand so we can touch hand to paw.

Other Side   Command that means heel on the right (rather than left) side.

Paws Up   Command that means lift both of your paws to the surface indicated, such as the arm of a chair.

positive reinforcements   Things the dog likes, including treats, toys, petting, and verbal praise.

praise   Verbal affirmation, approval, in a higher-than-normal tone of voice.

Release   Command that signals the end of an exercise.

Retrieve   Command that means bring back to me the item or toy that was thrown, or the item indicated.

Roll Over   Command that means roll your entire body over.

Roll Back   Command that means roll the other direction from roll over.

Say Your Prayers   Command that means lift your paws to the surface indicated, and then lower your head to your paws and hold still until released.

Shake   Command that means lift your right paw toward me so we can touch hand to paw.

Show Me Your Tummy   Command that means roll over onto your back and hold that position, baring your tummy.

Sit   Command that means lower the hips to the ground, keeping the front end up, and hold still.

Sit Pretty   Command that means sit up, balance on your hips and tail, and hold still.

socialization   The process of introducing a puppy to the world around him, including various people, sights, sounds, and smells.

Spin   Command that means turn in a small circle.

Stand   Command that means stand on all four paws and hold still.

Stand In Motion   Command that means stop moving forward and stand still.

Stay   Command that means hold this particular position until released.

target   Something used to cue that the dog will move or touch; to go from one place to another.

therapy dogs   Privately owned pets that are trained, evaluated, and certified to visit people who need some warmth and affection.

Touch   Command that means touch my hand or the item in my hand with your nose.

training tools   Anything that is used to train the dog, including the voice, leash, collar, treats, or toys.

trick training   The process of teaching tricks to your dog.

tricks   Actions or behavior your dog can do not normally taught as a part of obedience training; fun things.

Tug-of-War   A game with both parties (dog and owner) tugging on the toy.

Watch Me   Command that means pay attention and ignore distractions.

Wave   Command that means lift your paw up to shoulder height and move it up and down a few times.

Weave   Command that means weave through the indicated obstacles (poles, legs, hoops).

Appendix **B**

Resources

Dog Sports and Activities

Canada's Guide to Dog Sports

A listing of clubs and organizations in Canada.

www.canadasguidetodogs.com/clubs/activity

Dog Patch

Dog sports and activities.

www.dogpatch.org/dogs/shows.cfm

Working Dog Web

All about all dog sports.

www.workingdogweb.com

Acting

Animal Actors

Animal actors, agents, and extras.

www.animal-actors.com

Bash Dibra

Animal trainers.

www.starpet.com

Extras for Movies

Animal actors, casting calls, and more.

www.extrasformovies.com

Hollywood Paws

Detailed information on animal acting.

www.hollywoodpaws.com

Therapy Dog Organizations

Foundation for Pet Provided Therapy

A national organization evaluating and certifying dogs.

www.loveonaleash.org

The Delta Society

A multifaceted organization with a therapy dog division.

www.deltasociety.org

Therapy Dog International

An organization for evaluating and certifying dogs.

www.tdi-dog.org

Health

American Veterinary Medical Association

A great resource for animal health information.

www.avma.org/care4pets/

Herbs for Animals

Herbal remedies and information about them.

www.herbsforanimals.com

NetVet Veterinary Resources

Dr. Ken Boschert, Washington University, St. Louis, Missouri. A very informative site with breaking news in the veterinary field and animal health, career information, and much more.

netvet.wustl.edu

Dog Food Companies

California Natural

California Natural pet products.

www.naturapet.com

Canidae

Canidae Pet Foods

www.canidae.com

Honest Kitchen

The Honest Kitchen dehydrated foods.

www.thehonestkitchen.com

Natural Balance

Dick Van Patten's Natural Balance Pet Foods.

www.naturalbalanceinc.com

Old Mother Hubbard

Wellness dog foods.

www.oldmotherhubbard.com

Solid Gold

Solid Gold Health Products and pet foods.

www.solidgoldhealth.com

Wysong

Wysong pet foods.

www.wysong.net

Index

D

MDSA (Musical Dog Sport
  Association), 248
mixed-breed dogs, 57
mousers, 56
movements, freestyle dance, 242-246
movie dogs, 252-253
    agents, 259-262
    behavior, 254
    contracts, 265
    grooming, 254
    insurance, 265
    local opportunities, 258-259
    photographs, 263
    resumés, 263-265
    target training, 256-258
    training, 265-266
    tricks, 255
moving through the poles, Weave
  command, 109
multiple-dog routines, 221-222
music selection, freestyle dance, 241
Musical Canine Sports International.
  See MCSI
Musical Dog Sport Association. See
  MDSA
Musical Freestyle, 247

N

Name game, 145
    retrieving by name, 160-163
    leash, 166-168
    newspapers, 163-166
    taking items to someone,
      168-170
naming objects, 138
    Name game, 145
    personal things, 144
    toys, 138-143
negative reinforcement training, 16-17
newspapers
    Retrieve command, 163-166
    star dogs, 259

noisemakers, as training tools, 12
non-sporting dogs, 57

O

obedience training
    basic obedience commands, 7, 19
      Come command, 34
      Down command, 26-27
      Down Stay command, 28-29
      gaining attention of dog, 20-21
      Heel command, 32-34
      Release command, 23-24
      Sit command, 21
      Stay command, 24-26
      step-by-step approach, 20
      successful training tips, 35-36
      Watch Me command, 30-32
    intermediate obedience com-
      mands, 37
      off-leash skills, 45-48
      Retrieve command, 41-44,
        157-174
      Stand command, 38-40
      Stand In Motion command, 40
      training with distractions, 49-52
    knowing breed heritage, 54-57
    long-range goals, 59
    personality considerations, 58
    short-range goals, 60
    size considerations, 57-58
    tracking progress, 60-61
    trick training, 65
      Back command, 105-106
      bobbing for dog biscuits, 125
      Bow command, 84-85
      Crawl command, 72-75
      Dance command, 89
      Follow Me command, 106-108
      Give Kisses command, 121
      Go Right/Left command,
        122-124
      Go To Sleep command, 79-80